M

G

GREAT GAMBLING SCAMS

TRUE STORIES OF THE WORLD'S MOST AMAZING HUSTLERS

NIGEL GOLDMAN

JOHN BLAKE

Published by John Blake Publishing Ltd,
3 Bramber Court, 2 Bramber Road,
London W14 9PB, England

www.blake.co.uk

First published in paperback in 2007

ISBN: 978-1-84454-386-1

British Library Cataloguing-in-Publication Data:

A catalogue record for this book is available from the British Library.

Design by www.envydesign.co.uk

Printed in Great Britain by Bookmarque Ltd

1 3 5 7 9 10 8 6 4 2

Papers used by John Blake Publishing are natural, recyclable
products made from wood grown in sustainable forests. The manufacturing
processes conform to the environmental regulations
of the country of origin.

Every attempt has been made to contact the relevant copyright-holders,
but some were unobtainable. We would be grateful if the appropriate people
could contact us.

To Annie

Nigel Goldman was born in 1957 and educated at Carmel College, Oxon. He has traded in futures and precious metals in the City, owned a string of successful racehorses, run his own bookmaking business and is a keen poker player. He now lives in southern Spain with his girlfriend, appears regularly on TV and on the radio, acts and writes columns for various sport, financial and gambling magazines. This is his third book.

Contents

Author's Note   ix

1 The Man Who Broke The Bank   1
At Monte Carlo

2 Richard Marcus – The World's   23
Greatest Casino Cheat

3 The Flockton Grey Scandal   53

4 MIT Students Take On Vegas For Millions   69

5 The SkyBiz Multi-Million-Dollar   93
Internet Scam

6 The Malaysian Football Betting Scam   101

7 The £1 Million Ritz Casino Scam   117

8 The £10 Million Halifax IOU Thief   139

9 The Stock Exchange Insider-Dealing Scams   155

10 The Betting Exchange Conspiracies   165

11 The Financial Advisor With The
£2.3 Million Gambling Habit   181

12 Cheating At Poker   193

13 The Nigerian '419' Advance Fee Scam   211

Glossary Of Gambling Terms   221

Author's Note

Gambling has been around for centuries and has encompassed all walks of life. In the 18th and 19th centuries, the aristocracy famously enjoyed their flutters and some went spectacularly broke trying to beat the odds. More recently, a couple of financial advisors have been jailed after losing millions of pounds of clients' money backing outcomes unsuccessfully on the internet. And, while all this is going on, gambling cheats in all walks of life continue to conjure up new formulas to deprive their victims of their hard-earned cash.

The thing that strikes me about gambling is that it is all self-taught. If you want to learn languages, acting, singing, cooking or flower arranging, you'll find a plethora of choices of ways to go about it in your local paper, from private tuition to night classes. But gambling? No. You pick it up as you go along. Learn by your mistakes. Which makes cheating at it even more spectacular, because first you have to learn the rules, and then you have to learn how to break them.

In this book there are 13 true stories about some of the more spectacular gambling scams that have occurred all over the world over the past century or so. There is also a comprehensive glossary of gambling terminology at the end.

Enjoy. If you gamble already, it may well change the way you play. And, if you don't, it will put you on your guard before you do.

Bonne chance!

Nigel Goldman
Spain, 2007

owest level – in other words, a wager of
you lose a bet, you will move up to the
doubling the amount of the previous
of this system ensures that, whenever
eventually wins, you will win the amount
inal wager, in this instance one chip.
Martingale is extremely dangerous and
use occasionally long runs can occur
on even-money chances, and by the time
your 11th and 12th wager you are up to
048 units to try and recoup your original
s the unfortunate Mr Leigh found out, to
us cost, when he watched in horror as
up 13 times in a row, while he was betting
easing sums on red.

had not wiped himself out financially at
the casino had a trump card up their
had a table maximum, which he would
d on the very next spin anyway, to thwart
A story is told in *The Sealed Book of*
nich came out in 1924, that Arnold
once said to M. Blanc, manager of the
nte Carlo, 'Take off your maximum and
ainst you as long as you like.' Rothschild
ithout a maximum bet he could use the
ystem and eventually beat the house.
n't help poor Mr Leigh Sr, who didn't

The Man Who Broke The Bank At Monte Carlo

Nice is magnificently situated on the Baie des
Anges, surrounded by the foothills of the
Maritime Alps, some 19 miles from the Italian border.
It has a splendid old town, separated from the busy
new town by the river Paillon. With its sheltered
situation and mild climate, Nice is one of the oldest
established winter resorts on the Côte d'Azur, and is
also a very popular summer resort too. The old town
of Nice is a maze of narrow streets and lanes, dotted
with colourful cafes and restaurants. A flower
market is held every day on Cours Saleya. The 17th-
century cathedral has rich stucco decoration, fine
choir stalls and beautiful wood panelling in the

sacristy. This magnificent Baroque building was once the palace of the Counts of Castellar. It has a handsome entrance hall, an 18th-century pharmacy and ceiling paintings in the state apartments. The Jardin Albert 1er runs north-east from the sea front to the busy place Massena, the hub of the city's traffic, which is where the Fountain Du Soleil is situated. And the Casino Municipale.

When Norman Leigh first walked into the Casino Municipale with his father in the 1950s, I doubt he could have imagined the incredible sequence of events that was to be played out in that grand building over the following decade. That first visit to the casino ignited a touchpaper and started a chain of events so incredible that Norman Leigh has gone down in the history books of gambling as a legend, the man who orchestrated an event held as impossible by all expert opinion: breaking the bank at roulette.

This incredible gambling story started after Mr Leigh Sr, on that first visit to the Casino Municipale in Nice accompanied by his son, embarked on a disastrous betting adventure on the French roulette tables that was to see him financially ruined. Mr Leigh had fallen for the oldest trick in the book – gambling on the theory that even-chance bets on the outside chances at roulette must eventually come

good in one's favour. A
The hapless Mr Leigh
trying to break a seque
table. He kept doubling
panic, in large old Fren
an attempt to try to brea
chance coming up time

Betting systems are a
broad categories: bett
decision (known as flat b
wins (called positive
money after losses (cal
The negative progressio
Leigh employed. 'Labouc
correct names for this
bets after losses, and, wh
profitable in the short te
streak of bad luck can co

The origin of 'Marting
century. It is named af
English casino owner wh
losing punters to 'double
'Martingale' is one of t
using a negative progress
simple. The player uses a
as large as the preceding
64 etc. So long as you win

bet at the
one chip.
next wage
wager. Us
your wage
of the or
However,
risky, bec
against yo
you get to
1,024 and
one chip –
his enorm
black cam
in ever-in

Even if
that stag
sleeve. Th
have reac
his attac
Roulette,
Rothschi
casino in
I will pla
knew tha
Martinga
But this

The Man Who Broke The Bank At Monte Carlo

Nice is magnificently situated on the Baie des Anges, surrounded by the foothills of the Maritime Alps, some 19 miles from the Italian border. It has a splendid old town, separated from the busy new town by the river Paillon. With its sheltered situation and mild climate, Nice is one of the oldest established winter resorts on the Côte d'Azur, and is also a very popular summer resort too. The old town of Nice is a maze of narrow streets and lanes, dotted with colourful cafes and restaurants. A flower market is held every day on Cours Saleya. The 17th-century cathedral has rich stucco decoration, fine choir stalls and beautiful wood panelling in the sacristy. This magnificent Baroque building was once the palace of the Counts of Castellar. It has a handsome entrance hall, an 18th-century pharmacy and ceiling paintings in the state apartments. The Jardin Albert 1er runs north-east from the sea front to the busy place Massena, the hub of the city's traffic, which is where the Fountain Du Soleil is situated. And the Casino Municipale.

When Norman Leigh first walked into the Casino Municipale with his father in the 1950s, I doubt he could have imagined the incredible sequence of events that was to be played out in that grand building over the following decade. That first visit to the casino ignited a touchpaper and started a chain of events so incredible that Norman Leigh has gone down in the history books of gambling as a legend, the man who orchestrated an event held as impossible by all expert opinion: breaking the bank at roulette.

This incredible gambling story started after Mr Leigh Sr, on that first visit to the Casino Municipale in Nice accompanied by his son, embarked on a disastrous betting adventure on the French roulette tables that was to see him financially ruined. Mr Leigh had fallen for the oldest trick in the book – gambling on the theory that even-chance bets on the outside chances at roulette must eventually come good in one's favour. A very dangerous philosophy. The hapless Mr Leigh threw good money after bad trying to break a sequence of a run on the roulette table. He kept doubling up his wagers, almost in a panic, in large old French Franc casino plaques, in an attempt to try to break the house's run on an even chance coming up time and time again.

Betting systems are as old as the hills and fall into broad categories: betting the same after each decision (known as flat betting); raising wagers after wins (called positive progressions); and raising money after losses (called negative progressions). The negative progression was the system that Mr Leigh employed. 'Labouchere' or 'Martingale' are the correct names for this betting strategy of raising bets after losses, and, while this system can often be profitable in the short term, time and time again one streak of bad luck can completely wipe you out.

The origin of 'Martingale' dates back to the 18th century. It is named after Henry Martingale, an English casino owner who is reputed to have urged losing punters to 'double 'em up' with their wagers. 'Martingale' is one of the oldest betting systems using a negative progression, and the system is very simple. The player uses a betting series that is twice as large as the preceding one, as with 1, 2, 4, 8, 16, 32, 64 etc. So long as you win a bet, you will continue to bet at the lowest level – in other words, a wager of one chip. If you lose a bet, you will move up to the next wager, doubling the amount of the previous wager. Use of this system ensures that, whenever your wager eventually wins, you will win the amount of the original wager, in this instance one chip. However, Martingale is extremely dangerous and risky, because occasionally long runs can occur against you on even-money chances, and by the time you get to your 11th and 12th wager you are up to 1,024 and 2,048 units to try and recoup your original one chip – as the unfortunate Mr Leigh found out, to his enormous cost, when he watched in horror as black came up 13 times in a row, while he was betting in ever-increasing sums on red.

Even if he had not wiped himself out financially at that stage, the casino had a trump card up their sleeve. They had a table maximum, which he would have reached on the very next spin anyway, to thwart his attack. A story is told in *The Sealed Book of Roulette*, which came out in 1924, that Arnold Rothschild once said to M. Blanc, manager of the casino in Monte Carlo, 'Take off your maximum and I will play against you as long as you like.' Rothschild knew that without a maximum bet he could use the Martingale system and eventually beat the house. But this didn't help poor Mr Leigh Sr, who didn't

4

even have the cab fare back to the hotel, let alone the means to get himself and his son back to the UK. Young Norman would never forget the smug look of self-satisfaction on the face of the chubby young casino manager as he stood by the roulette table in his black dinner jacket and bow tie, arms folded, having wiped out the Englishman. It was a look that was to haunt him for years to come.

As if the casino manager's smirk wasn't bad enough, Norman then had to suffer the indignity of attending the British Consulate in Nice that very evening and listening to his father tell a pack of lies to the officials there – that they had been robbed at knifepoint by French peasants at the roadside, and needed their fare home and some pocket money provided for them. The helplessness, poverty, despair and humiliation remained deeply engraved on Norman Leigh's mind and, as soon as they returned to England courtesy of the British Consulate, he dedicated himself to formulating a plan that would enable him to exact his revenge on the Casino Municipale in Nice. He did not care how long it took. Revenge would be sweet, and worth waiting for.

Over the following years, Norman Leigh turned himself into an extraordinary man. Despite having no formal education, he taught himself to speak six or seven languages fluently. He loved taking risks, just like his father – hence his interest in gambling. He always dressed smartly, wore a suit with a white shirt, bow tie or cravat, and – importantly – had an agile mind when it came to mathematics. The size and speed of his father's loss at the casino in Nice continued to torture his mind, yet he was convinced that there must be a method or system he could devise that would enable him to recover all the money, and more. And so Norman Leigh devoted the bulk of his time in playing around with roulette systems and methods, spending endless hours in casinos and practising on the life-size roulette wheel he had at home. He felt certain in the back of his mind that there must be a method or strategy that could put the house in the same unfortunate position as the punter when a long run or sequence occurred, causing the bank to participate in the role of the player and have *them* hoping for a break in the run. And, of course, being forced to pay out, just as his father had to, as long as the run continued. How wonderful it would be, he thought, to reach the house limit on a winning streak!

He believed strongly that such a system could be devised, and spent hours experimenting with various staking plans and strategies, but one of the problems he faced was that there were six even-money options on a roulette table, so how was he to choose which one the run would occur on? It could be red or black, high or low, odd or even. One thing struck home during the hundreds of hours of practice spins on his wheel at home. He noted that long sequences – or imbalances, as he preferred to call them – occurred with incredible regularity on many of the even chances. But he had to devise a way of being able to capitalise on such a run, or imbalance, while at the same time protecting his bankroll should such a run not occur. Risk versus reward ratio, to put it bluntly.

For the bulk of the early 1960s, Norman Leigh spent over fifty hours a week practising and refining roulette-staking disciplines. He supported himself during this period by playing roulette for real money, and having the odd bet on a horse or dog he'd received inside information about from his gambling cronies. While he found some success with various perms and systems he devised, he couldn't convince himself that he had perfected a strategy that would see him through to his final goal, a goal he had now decided simply had to be achieved and which took over enormous importance in his life.

By 1965, he was almost there. But there was still one vital ingredient missing. He had now established – through thousands of practice spins, which he had meticulously logged – that there were indeed long series of imbalances on the even chances at roulette: runs of high numbers outnumbering lows, long streaks of blacks outnumbering reds, large percentages of odds over evens. But he still couldn't fathom out a staking discipline to take advantage of these imbalances efficiently. Maybe the great Albert Einstein had been right when he said, 'The only way to win at roulette is to steal the money when the dealer isn't looking.' But Norman Leigh wasn't to be put off.

One day, in the spring of 1965, he decided to go for a stroll to clear his head, and try and think the whole thing through calmly. It was while he was out, taking in the fresh air, that he went back in his mind to the cause of his father's downfall at roulette all those years earlier. He theorised that the reason so many players lose with 'Labouchere' is that they run into the house limits, or lose their playing capital, and are unable to recoup losses. Since the bank has almost unlimited capital in comparison to the players, the bank can out-wait most player assaults, knowing that either the house betting limit or the player's own limited financial resources will bring about the player's demise. The Labouchere system was first discovered by Henry Labouchere, an English gambler who travelled the world playing it until he died in 1912. It was the Labouchere system that had caused his father's downfall, as it meant investing higher and higher amounts, spin by spin, to recoup the losses. Why was it not possible, he wondered, to put the house in the position of 'Labouchere', where they had to keep paying out during the run of imbalance? Runs, he was now quite convinced, were not abnormal. Surely he could build a staking discipline that took advantage of these imbalances?

His mind kept wandering back to that Labouchere staking method that had been so costly. And then he got it, in a flash of inspiration. If the Labouchere system was the dangerous and expensive culprit, all he had to do was create a staking system that was the *opposite* of Labouchere. Or an inversion of it. Leigh reasoned that a reverse-betting strategy was the approach that would most closely resemble the bank's approach to most other players. He would wait out the small losses until a large win occurred. He rushed back to his home and grabbed his working papers. The solution had been staring him in the face for months. The Reverse Labouchere system was born, and Norman Leigh just couldn't wait to put what he had discovered to the test.

The Reverse Labouchere roulette system begins with a series of numbers – any you want to use – with each number representing the chip amount you are going to risk. Norman Leigh started with 1-2-3-4-5-6, but later refined it to 1-2-3-4. The size of your wager will always be the sum of the outside two numbers. So in the first example the bet would be 7 chips, and in the second – the one Leigh stuck to – it would be 5. The beauty of the Reverse Labouchere is that, when the bet wins, the size of the wager is added to the end of the sequence, in the first example 7, and the next bet would be for 8 units (1 plus 7). But – and here was the Achilles heel to roulette that Norman Leigh had unwittingly uncovered – if the bet lost, you crossed out two numbers from your sequence from either end, and the next bet became the total of the outside two numbers left. In the first example, then, if the first bet had lost, the numbers 1 and 6 would be crossed out, and the next bet would become 7 units (2 plus 5), and, if this won, a 7 would be added, and if it lost the 2 and 5 would be crossed out. This betting pattern would continue until either all the numbers had been crossed out, in which case you started again, or until such time as the progression lasted until the house limit was reached. When this natural winning streak occurred, the Reverse Labouchere staking system would have dictated maximum payout, and the player would then take down the final winning bet, realising a huge profit (around 6,000 units).

Leigh got out his scribblings of series of roulette

numbers he had experienced in real life both in casinos and at home on his practice wheel. He started applying the staking system to the six even-chance outside bets, and added and reduced his stakes according to the outcome of the spin. While there were certain draw downs, and – frustratingly – progressions that looked promising often fizzled out, he was encouraged to see that on several occasions progressions carried on right the way to the mythical table maximum, culminating in a massive payout that more than made up for any of the small and inevitable losses. He spent the next few weeks spinning the wheel, placing the chips and working the Reverse Labouchere system until he was satisfied and convinced that it worked. And work it did: over the course of 100 sessions, 96 were profitable, and some winning sessions were extremely profitable.

Norman Leigh had three problems with the system, though. First, how would he handle the staking plan when a zero came up? Until now he had simply ignored it and carried on, but the more he thought about it, the more he decided it was beneficial in the long run to count it as a half result, and make up the balance of the chips to the correct bet. Casinos remove half your stake from an even-money bet when zero comes up. The second, and more serious problem, was how to physically handle the Reverse Labouchere betting system in a live casino. At home on his practice wheel, he had plenty of time to calculate and place his bets on the six even-money chances, but he was painfully aware that in the real hustle and bustle of a casino that would not be possible. And, third, how would he finance the operation? He went to bed that evening feeling rather dejected, but woke up the following morning with a brilliant idea. He would recruit 12 players, show them the system and take them to France with him to beat the casino. He would even ask them to bankroll the operation, and he would take his cut of the action. That morning, Norman Leigh placed a classified advert in the following day's edition of the *Evening Standard*, and waited for his phone to ring.

The response was phenomenal. He got responses from people of all walks of life, from different backgrounds and of different age and sex. Out-of-work actors and actresses, a struck-off accountant, a retired schoolteacher. The list was endless. By the end of the week, he had arranged a series of meetings at his home, where he would demonstrate the system to his new recruits, and then carefully select the 12 he would bring with him to France to take on the Casino Municipale in Nice.

Each time potential candidates arrived at Norman's home for interview, he took them into his room, where the roulette table was set up, and lectured them like a schoolmaster. He took this mission extremely seriously, and he had no room on board for passengers. Some fell by the wayside there and then; others became even more interested. By the middle of 1966, Norman Leigh had his team together, they were sufficiently bankrolled and Norman noted with satisfaction that they all entrusted him with their stake money, which he would change slowly over a period of time in the West End into French Francs. They agreed that, as the scheme was his brainchild, Norman would keep 50 per cent of the profits after expenses.

The team spent weeks practising the Reverse Labouchere system on his home roulette table until they had the staking discipline absolutely perfected and spot on. Norman decided that they would go to France and play for ten days, with two teams of six on each roulette table, each playing the staking system at the same time on odd, even, red, black, high and low, with him as an overseer in charge to make sure everything went according to plan. As the casino staff would swiftly uncover the team, with their notepads for writing down the progressions and their unusual betting patterns, he decided that he would inform the casino management that he had devised a system that he believed would win at roulette, and ask if they had any objection to him trying it out and using it. This was a gamble worth taking, as he knew the management would welcome them with open arms. He also knew, deep down, that they would beat the casino.

In the summer of 1966, Norman Leigh took his team of 12 to Nice. They checked into a hotel near to the casino, and dined in a restaurant together the same evening. There, Norman Leigh delivered his last lecture to the group. The very next night, they were going to the Casino Municipale to put the Reverse Labouchere roulette staking plan to test, and, if all went well, they would be doing the same for the next nine nights as well. Norman Leigh handed out 12 manila envelopes to his team; each was crammed with their stake money in French Francs.

Over a decade after leaving the casino with his father, both of them with tails between their legs, Norman Leigh led his team to the Casino Municipale in Nice. Norman Leigh's heart missed a beat as he entered the glitzy surroundings, but not because of the extra tables that had been installed, or the redecoration, or the bustle of the gaming floor. It was because of the casino manager he set eyes upon, chubby and resplendent in his dinner jacket, arms folded, just as he had been all those years earlier. Norman Leigh screwed his eyes up and looked at him with pure malice, took a gulp, hoped he wasn't recognised and went straight over to him. 'I believe I have discovered a betting system that can beat your casino at roulette. I have brought a team of 12 players with me from England, and, if you have no objections, I would like to put my system to the test at your casino.'

The manager, who had heard it all before, let out a small chuckle and welcomed these new punters with open arms. He never even gave Leigh a cursory glance and, if he had, he wouldn't have recognised him anyway. Over the years, he had taken great pleasure in watching a host of English punters go bankrupt in his casino. Norman Leigh's team headed for two empty roulette tables, got out their pads and pencils, and started work.

Almost as a mirror image to their weeks of preparation, nothing much happened for the first couple of hours. A small progression on odd fizzled out on one table, and on the other a similar streak on red was thwarted just as it was about to mushroom. Norman Leigh, meanwhile, was hovering between the two tables, keeping an eye on everyone, and making sure nobody was uncomfortable or panicking, and that the crib cards were keeping the staking plan accurate.

One of the bizarre features that Norman Leigh had noticed about the Reverse Labouchere system was that a progression that fizzled out just as it started looking promising often reappeared and got going again with gusto shortly afterwards. And that was what happened on the first roulette table with odd. The man playing odd was a retired schoolteacher from Epsom, one of the stronger and more reliable members of Norman's team, and one that he had selected from the early batch of applicants. All of a sudden, odd started unbalancing even quite dramatically, and the bets were becoming substantial. Norman looked over the teacher's shoulder to see the progression on his pad, which now looked like this: 606, 744, 882, 1,068, 1,254, 1,512, 1,770, 2,100, 2,430, 2,760, 3,162, 3,564, 4,018, 4,522, 5,026. The next wager would be 5,626 units, approaching the table maximum, and, if that one obliged, the streak on odd would have run its course, and the player would draw down his winnings and start all over again with a bet of just five units. By now there was a small crowd of onlookers at the table, in awe of the towers of chips and plaques in front of the schoolteacher. 'Fait vaux jeux.' The dealer spun the wheel. The little white ivory ball spun round and round and clanked into a slot with number 11 on it. 'Onze, noir, impair.' Just over three hours after walking into the Casino Municipale, the first progression had climaxed, netting the team a substantial win. The schoolteacher neatly stacked up his high-value winning plaques, and then staked the minimum, five units, on odd, just as he had been taught.

Meanwhile, on the other table, a similar progression was taking place on the low numbers. Norman wandered over to observe. This time it was the turn of the out-of-work actress to be the centre of attention as the low numbers prevailed. A second mushroom climaxed with almost the same ease as the first, and the team had hit the house limit twice within the space of a few minutes. They carried on playing for about another hour, during which nothing much of note happened, all the even chances balancing each other out. Norman then gave the signal to cash in and leave, and meet him in his suite at the hotel. He hurried up to his rooms, and pulled six bottles of chilled champagne out of the fridge; he hadn't believed in his wildest dreams that he would be celebrating this quickly. Two successful progressions on the first day! The team arrived, all in a jolly mood, and spilled their French Francs out on to the bed. Norman poured the champagne as they counted the large bundles of French banknotes into neat stacks. They had won the equivalent of $18,500. Norman took his half and shared the balance out among the other team members, who were absolutely thrilled at the ease of their tax-free gains.

The following night, they were back at work in the casino. Nothing happened. They drew a blank on night three as well, which was probably just as well, because what happened on night four was quite extraordinary. Literally the minute they sat down at the tables, a progression started on red, quickly followed by one on even on the other table. Within a quarter of an hour, both progressions had maxed out, and another took over on high on the first table. This one matured as well, and by now, with the team having hit three successful mushrooms in less than an hour, the casino management started taking a little more interest in them. 'Your system seems to be working well, Monsieur, but we have seen these things before. You'll give it all back in time.' How wrong they were, as the team went on to have the most successful night ever, culminating in five successful winning streaks, and winning over $50,000.

On night five, the casino started playing tricks on the team. Shills – players employed by the house – were used to crowd the teams at the table, and take their seats during toilet breaks. Croupiers were told to spin the ball quickly when a progression was in progress to put the players off, and not allow them sufficient time to calculate the next bet and place the wager. Waiters were instructed to spill coffee on the laps of team members that were placing large bets. But none of this thwarted the efforts of Norman Leigh's team, who were now driven by adrenalin, and the lure of plenty of tax-free Francs courtesy of the casino. They actually only hit one progression that night over a period of six-and-a-half hours of play, but that was soon made up for on night six, when two more came in. By the tenth night, the team were up the equivalent of over $160,000, and the casino were giving them some serious heat. Just as a progression was getting going, the casino manager came over to the table and closed it down there and then, in the middle of play. The staff draped a black cloth over the table, and the manager then did the same thing on the other table that the team were playing on. The game was over and the team was made to leave.

Although the casino had closed the table, they had still suffered a very substantial loss indeed, and, as the casinos in France were government-owned at the time, the French government was obliged to bail the Municipale out (it also ejected the team from the country). Norman Leigh had well and truly had his revenge. He and his team arrived back in England over $160,000 richer, amid a blaze of publicity in the English press. A book was written about the episode, and Leigh became a cause célèbre among the roulette players of the world.

Would the Reverse Labouchere system work today, in a modern casino? Remember that Norman Leigh and his team were playing in Monte Carlo in the mid-1960s. They were allowed to play without too much interference and heat for the first few nights, and they were also playing in games where the minimum to maximum betting spreads were huge, which was necessary to make his approach work.

I first discovered the Reverse Labouchere system in the late 1970s and put it to the test, on my own, in a Birmingham casino. Instead of using a team of six at the table, I covered the even-money outside chances on my own, but, instead of backing all six as Norman Leigh's team did, I simply subtracted the differences, and covered just three, high odd and black. One needs a very versatile mathematical mind to achieve this. Despite the casino trying every trick to put me off my stride – changing dealer after every spin, spinning short and generally giving me heat – I enjoyed one long progression, on odd, which took me to the table maximum. I won £9,000.

The following night, eager to repeat my performance, I returned – to find myself barred from the casino. It seemed that English casinos, at any rate, considered the system at least as dangerous to them as card counting at blackjack. Still, I bought a 1973 mustard-yellow Porsche Carrera Targa – registration EEB 2 – with my Reverse Labouchere winnings, so I wasn't that put out!

I have recently tested Norman Leigh's system against a database of real roulette results and found that it still works. But, for the Reverse Labouchere system to perform consistently, betting spreads of up to 1–2,000 need to be found, for example, a roulette table with $5 minimum and $10,000 maximum on the outside even chances. These can still be found in certain casinos in the world, but the negatives must also be pointed out, too: Norman Leigh and his team could play with starting units of only 25 cents; today we must start with $5 in most casinos. A bankroll of around $15,000 to $20,000 would be required. The play is very obvious to casino personnel and incredible perseverance is required. I've heard about a few teams operating today who have duplicated Norman Leigh's system successfully. But one word of advice: don't try this on casino sites on the internet. The system only works on real roulette tables. This is because of the theory that no roulette wheel is mechanically perfect and is therefore subject to biases in certain sectors, or towards certain numbers. It could well be these biases help make the Reverse Labouchere system the one that allows the player to beat the house at roulette.

After his success in Monte Carlo, Norman Leigh lived like a prince, but sadly squandered his winnings and died like a pauper some years ago, alcoholic and alone in a bed-sit. I wonder if any of his team members are still around. Whatever the dismal circumstances of his demise, Norman Leigh deserves high praise for discovering and refining the Reverse Labouchere method, and employing it to devastating effect against his lifelong enemy, the Casino Municipale in Nice.

Richard Marcus – The World's Greatest Casino Cheat

Richard Marcus readily admits that he was hooked on gambling from a very early age. The incredible roller-coaster ride culminating in his becoming, without doubt, the greatest casino cheat ever started years earlier in elementary school, where he started flipping baseball cards with his school mates. As he had accumulated the biggest collection of baseball cards in the neighbourhood, housed in 20 shoeboxes, his collection became the target of his crooked schoolboy peers, who were determined to relieve him of his prized collection no matter what. It was there that he first learned about cheating at gambling.

The baseball cards had coloured banners on them depicting the player's name and team logo, with two teams sharing one colour. When these kids flipped cards, the cards were held face down, and each turned the top card over. Whoever matched the colour of the previous card won. Then they started playing for serious stakes: whoever matched ten colours won a huge pile of cards. Richard lost his whole baseball-card collection flipping over a couple of days, but soon realised that he had been cheated out of it. His school friends had gone to the amazing lengths of memorising all the teams, players and colours on every single card. When it was Richard's turn to call, and they saw he was calling correctly, they simply held the top card in place and pulled out the one in second place underneath. Because of this sleight of hand, Richard couldn't win any pots, and his precious baseball-card collection passed into the hands of his cheating peers. This very first experience of gambling changed Richard's life forever, making him determined to be on the side of the cheaters rather than a victim, and turned him from adolescent baseball-card collector to grown-up thief.

By the age of 13, Richard was missing school classes regularly, and was already involved playing in poker games downtown and visiting the track when he should have been in class. He needed a constant supply of cash to finance his gambling, both at cards and at the track, and was not averse to pulling off the odd con or two. One of his favourites in those early days was a trick he had picked up from a movie. He would send one of his trusted mates into a candy store to buy some chocolate for around 50 cents, and got them to pay for it with a $20 bill on which Richard had drawn a little heart in crayon next to the presidential portrait. Once his friend had come out of the store with the change of the twenty, Richard went into the store next. He would also buy some candy, and pay for it with a dollar bill. When the shopkeeper had placed the note in his cash register, and paid Richard the change for the dollar, Richard would go into a well-rehearsed song-and-dance routine, insisting he had paid with a $20 bill and demanding change from it. He would then deliver his coup de grace: 'I know I paid you with a twenty, and I can prove it. My grandmother gave me that $20 bill last night and drew a little heart on it in crayon.' Of course, the shopkeeper would go back to the till, pull out the top $20 bill in the cash drawer, see the heart on it that Richard had described, and melt. Richard got his 19-odd dollars in change – and a free candy bar. By his early teens he had palled up with an Italian boy called Paul who came from a Mafia family and they must have pulled this one off a thousand times all over Bergen County and New York. They used candy stores, delis and even busy supermarkets to pull their ruse. Their well-practised routine earned them plenty of cash, as did the next scam Richard figured out, one that they would put into force the minute they had learned how to drive...

Four years later, Paul drove his new GTO into a filling station and asked the attendant to fill it up. Paying for the gas with a $100 bill, and making certain he flashed the cash so the attendant saw the wad it had been peeled from, Paul went into his newly rehearsed routine: 'Jesus, my dad's gonna kill me. I know I had it on ten minutes ago.'

'What?' the attendant enquired.

'My diamond ring. My dad bought it for me for my 18th birthday yesterday, and now I've lost the fucking thing.'

'That's life,' came the casual reply.

'It's probably worth a couple of grand. But that's not the issue, it's the sentimental value that counts.' Then Paul got into his shiny car and started the engine, before leaning out of the window, almost as an afterthought, to deliver the crucial line. 'Look, I doubt I lost the ring here in this filling station, but should it turn up I will give you $500 reward for its

26

return. I'll be watching the Giants game at McCann's over the road.'

Richard left it an hour or so, and then pulled up to the same gas station in a beat-up Chevy. 'Five dollars' worth, please,' he said, handing the attendant an assortment of loose change, dropping a few coins as he did so. On bending down to retrieve the change, bingo! He stood up with Paul's lost ring in his hand. 'Look what I've found. Do you reckon it's worth anything?'

The attendant took the ring and examined it carefully. 'It's probably a cubic. I can't believe anyone losing a real diamond in a filling station.'

'Yeah, you're probably right, no sweat, I'll give it to a girl if I get lucky and pull.'

Now the attendant got interested. 'I could give you a little money for it if you like?'

'How much?'

'I dunno, twenty bucks?'

'Twenty bucks! You gotta be kiddin'. Even the cheapest cubics cost more than that! And, anyway, the bloody thing could be real, and it's massive.'

The attendant had been sucked in. 'OK, how much do you want for it, then?'

'A couple of hundred at least.'

'Wait here,' the attendant said. 'I'll make a quick call from inside, see if my pal is interested, see if we can do a deal.'

At McCann's, where the Giants game was on the TV, the barman answered the phone. 'Anyone in here lost a ring at the Texaco garage down the road?'

Paul took the call.

'Hey, I've found your ring.'

'Brilliant, I'll be right there.'

The attendant came back outside to Richard. 'I'll tell you what,' he said, 'I can go a hundred on it.'

They settled on $150. Richard took the cash and met Paul on a roadside hill overlooking the Texaco garage. From the comfort of Paul's air-conditioned GTO, they took turns in watching the attendant pacing up and down the garage forecourt, looking at his watch. After about ten minutes, he couldn't take it any more, jumped into his own car and sped over to McCann's. The duo followed him and, when he emerged from McCann's, realising he had been conned, Paul and Richard roared by in the GTO, and Paul yelled 'Asshole!' out of the window.

They repeated the gas station scam many times, almost always collecting.

When Richard Marcus drove to Las Vegas in his new Mustang convertible in the summer of 1976, a few days before his 21st birthday, I doubt even he could have imagined how his life was about to pan out. Courtesy of a substantial touch he had landed at

Saratoga racetrack a week earlier, the new wheels also had twenty grand in cash stashed in the boot. Richard couldn't wait to step inside one of the upmarket casinos he had heard so much about over the past few years – unbelievably, despite having gambled every day for the past decade, he had never actually set foot inside a casino.

His first port of call in Vegas was the showy and glitzy Riviera Hotel, where he took a suite, and spent the next few days playing high-stakes baccarat with his twenty-grand bankroll. To start with, he did rather well, turning his twenty grand into fifty, and then into a hundred. The casino, keen to massage the ego of their new young high-roller, comped everything, from the suite to expensive dinners in their best restaurants, and endless rivers of champagne. And, as they had seen happen a million times before, the casino's investment in pampering paid off. On the day of his 21st birthday, Richard Marcus blew the whole lot. The following day, he sold his prized Mustang convertible and promptly gambled away all that money too.

He was now absolutely broke, literally penniless, and the Riviera caught on to this fact pretty quickly too, turfing him out of his $800-a-night suite after noticing he hadn't wagered a single bet for a couple of days. Richard ended up on the Strip, and it was scorching, over 100 degrees outside in Vegas during the day. He soon discovered how much he had taken the comfort of air conditioning for granted as he pounded the streets, looking for somewhere to shelter, forced to eat in cheap coffee shops and run out without paying the bill. The night after sleeping in the luxury of the $800-a-night hotel suite, he bedded down below the I-15 overpass, in the company of druggies and winos. That was to be his home for the next ten days. In the mornings, he slipped into hotel pool areas and used the outside bathrooms to wash and shave with toiletries he stole from the hotel's trolleys. Then he ate in all the hotel coffee shops, each time walking out without paying.

Richard was starting to get worn out by this existence. Figuring he would have to get a job to stay sane, he started to make enquiries about how one got a position in the casinos as a croupier; he had realised that, as gambling was all he knew about, he would have to take up employment on the other side of the table, at least for the time being. He quickly learned that to find a job in the hotels and casinos on the main part of the Strip meant attending croupier school and passing tests. He couldn't wait that long, so decided instead to settle for the trashier casinos downtown, where you could literally walk in and get started as a 'shill' – a casino employee who sits at the card tables and plays with the house's money. The idea is to keep all the tables in action during slack periods, so that when real punters walk in there are always games in progress, and not empty tables with bored croupiers standing behind them.

After several dry runs and knock-backs, Richard got lucky and was offered the job of a shill in a downtown, downmarket dump of a casino called the Four Queens. Mercifully, his life as a bum and coffee-shop renegade was over. Soon he was practising dealing games, and a month later he was promoted to dealing blackjack, mini-baccarat and roulette at the Four Queens. He started in the graveyard shift from midnight to eight in the morning, before being transferred to the swing shift that ran from six o'clock at night to two in the morning.

Over the next few months as a swing dealer, Richard got to know all the gambling junkies, addicts and degenerates. A pathological gambler called Whackey was one of the regular patrons. He used to come into the Four Queens every night at nine, always overly refreshed, and had been doing so as long as anyone remembered. The only culture associated with Whackey was to be found under his nails.

One night, he told Richard his story – which, unbelievably, turned out to be true. Whackey was a bum who spent the day begging on the Strip, and the nights emptying his pockets in grotty bars on cheap spirits, and at the Four Queens where he played slots and a bit of roulette, finances permitting. One night just before Christmas ten years earlier, Whackey had arrived at the Four Queens a little earlier than usual as it was raining, promptly emptied his pockets into the slots and lost. He then marched over to his favourite roulette table, and placed a folded-up dollar bill on number 4. The dealer spun the wheel, and the ball landed on number 4. Whackey won $35. Keeping his lucky dollar bill, which he put back in his pocket, he let his bet ride. Number 4 repeated, and Whackey now had $1,225. He wanted to let it ride again, but the casino maximum was $100, and Whackey bitched at this and reduced the bet to the $100. Number 4 came in a third time in a row, and Whackey now had $4,725. The casino manager pulled the croupier off the wheel, and installed another, meaner one. That didn't put Whackey off one iota. He not only won again, but number 4 came up an incredible fifth time as well. Whackey's five-time win on roulette is still Las Vegas's official record on an honest roulette wheel. The casino had no hesitation in calling in the Nevada Gaming Board the following morning to examine the wheel to ensure it had not been tampered with – which it had not.

But Whackey wasn't finished yet. Not by a long

chalk. He took his $12,000 in roulette profits to the blackjack table and placed a $1,000 chip on all seven betting stations. As only a single card deck was in use, the four blackjacks he got that first round was the maximum possible. Whackey went on an incredible winning run. The Four Queens kept changing dealers and plying him with more whisky to break his run, but Whackey kept winning and winning. He was ahead three hundred grand when he hit the craps table, and there he shot the dice for an incredible two hours. By the time it was all over, Whackey had the Four Queens beat for an incredible million dollars, at which point, he literally fell into the craps table, intoxicated and exhausted. In a panic, the casino manager coaxed Whackey into the best suite, and put his million in the casino cage for safekeeping, but not that lucky $1 bill which had started his incredible roll. Whackey took it up to his suite and put it safely under his pillow.

Unfortunately, waking up the next day as a millionaire – and realising he didn't have to go back on the streets begging – sadly proved to be poor Whackey's downfall. Having nothing better to do, he went back into the casino, where it took him a whole week to blow the entire million dollars. Before kicking him out of his suite and on to the strip, the casino manager offered him $100 for the lucky one-dollar bill that remained in his pocket. Whackey refused. The next night, he was arrested in the Four Queens Hotel gift shop for stealing a candy bar that cost a dollar.

After he finished his story, Richard asked him why he didn't simply pay for the candy bar with the dollar bill. He should have known the answer, it was simple, really. That was his lucky dollar, and there was no way the Four Queens was getting it.

Richard had also experienced the few punters who tried to bribe him to turn the tables against the house. Dealers are vulnerable to this, being persuaded to flash their hole card at blackjack, or overpay a winning bet. Richard was having none of that. But, one night in June 1977, a man who was going to change his life forever sat down at his mini-baccarat table.

It was late in the shift, and Richard's table was dead. A very handsome man in his mid-forties, casually but stylishly dressed, sat down at the table and changed up a hundred dollars. He seemed more interested in small talk than the cards. They exchanged stories about places they both knew in Manhattan, and Richard confided in him his story about how he had ended up being a dealer at the Four Queens. Richard immediately liked the man, and felt comfortable and impressed with him. At the end of the shift, the man suggested that Richard meet him for a drink at the Horseshoe Casino bar. Richard, never having socialised with a customer before, sensed something important was about to happen, and agreed. And that was how Richard Marcus met Joe Classon, Las Vegas's smartest cheat.

Binion's Horseshoe was considered one of Vegas's smartest joints. It was a no-limit casino, and people could – and did – make bets of a million dollars on the throw of a dice or the turn of a card. It was also home to the newly started World Series of Poker. Over cocktails, Joe sussed Richard out. 'I've been watching you deal baccarat for the past week, but you wouldn't have seen me. None of the floormen at the Four Queens has the slightest idea what goes on at the baccarat tables, yet you didn't nick a dime. Why's that?'

'No reason, nothing much worth stealing, really. I only got chosen to deal the baccarat because I was the only one in there who understood the rules.'

Joe was quite right, baccarat had only recently been installed at the Four Queens, and the bulk of the personnel and punters didn't even know the basic rules. And some of the crew were stealing small-value chips and getting away with it. Richard had not been tempted, though – memories of those ten nights under the freeway were still fresh in his mind. Richard was impressed with Joe's knowledge of the casino, although, no matter how hard he tried, he couldn't picture seeing him in there before that night. He felt sure, though, that Joe was going to make a move on him at any minute, an illegal move to rob the casino, and somehow Richard felt that the more he heard from his new friend, the more he was going to go for it.

'So, where do you see yourself a year or two from now? Not still dealing in that shit hole across the road, surely?'

'Nah, I'm just waiting for the right move to come along, I suppose,' Richard replied.

'Suppose I was to give you a push in the right direction, so to speak?' Joe now fixed Richard's gaze with his own, firmly and confidently.

Richard downed his drink in one, shook Joe's hand, and agreed there and then to be part of his team. All he had to do now was come up with a worthwhile scam at the Four Queens, and turn his back on his career as a croupier. He was in; there was now no turning back.

When Richard next met Joe ten days later, it was in his suite at the Tropicana Hotel, and he had the scheme completely worked out. In Joe's suite were his two associates, Duke and Jerry. Duke was in his mid-thirties, and had baby-blue eyes, while Jerry had the look of an American football player. They were passing round a joint, but Richard didn't smoke, so he got straight down to business, and divulged his plan.

'About ten minutes before the end of my shift at two in the morning, I want Joe to come and sit on my baccarat table and play in $100 black chips. That will set him up as a big player for the few hands that are left before I hand over to the next dealer on the graveyard shift. Now, here's the key: it is my job to shuffle the cards and place them in the baccarat shoe before the new dealer gets to the table. I am going to set up the deck during the shuffle with as many winning player hands as I can, and let Joe know before I leave the table how many there are going to be. Joe will have to keep an eye on the floorman while I am doing the shuffling and lacing the cards, to make sure he is not taking too much notice, but, from experience, at that time in the morning, on a quiet table he rarely does. As soon as I am gone, and the new dealer comes on, you guys, who have already been in the casino for a while getting noticed as big hitters on the dice and roulette, come and sit down at the table and bet the maximum on the player until the run is over. After that, in order to avoid suspicion, play a mixture of bank and player to almost equal sums of money, so the worst you can lose is the bit of tax, and stay there until the shoe is over. If I can get five or six player hands in the shoe, it will be a good night's work. And the beauty of it is, if the Four Queens think they have been burned, they will assume it must have been the fault of the graveyard dealer, not me, as I will already be gone.'

The room had gone quiet, and Joe's three new accomplices in crime sat with their mouths wide open.

'What about the burn card?' Joe asked.

'Quite right, I forgot. I will try and make the top card a deuce, so that the dealer has to burn two cards. Be careful to make sure that she burns two, not one or three; many dealers make a basic mistake on the burn. So, when I give Joe the signal after the shuffle I will say two, six. This means that the top card is a deuce, two cards will be burned, and there will be six winning player hands. Of course, if I can't force a deuce to the top, I may say five, five, but, whatever I say, if the top card that comes out isn't the one I mentioned, something's gone wrong and the whole thing is off.'

They spent the next few hours going through it all, and decided to get four more players involved so that they could cover all seven boxes, at $500 a box, netting themselves $3,500 a hand. Duke and Jerry had their girlfriends coming over, and Joe had a couple of other trustees in mind. It was decided that all seven would enter the casino at different times and from separate entrances, and change up sufficient money at blackjack, roulette and craps to ensure that the casino saw them as big players before they even hit the baccarat table.

Part two – the winning series of bets – was easy, but part three – getting out – was more difficult. Joe elaborated on Richard's theory: 'If us seven continue to play after the coup until the shoe is over, betting roughly equal sums on the player and the bank, we will probably lose a little back, but we will keep the bulk of the thousands we have stung them for. That will be worth it, and the casino will see us as big players, even though they can't win back what we have had them over for. In other words, they won't even realise they've been robbed.' The scene was set for the following Saturday evening. The Four Queens was about to get fleeced.

Upon shuffling the baccarat cards for possibly the last time in his career, Richard decided to try and put as many hands together as he could for his team. Joe was signalling – by gently rubbing his chin with his thumb and forefinger – that Harold, the floorman, had his back to him, and Richard quickly got a deuce and two dead cards, followed by four natural hands together. Then he managed to put in three more winning hands for the player, all unnoticed. By the time he had finished shuffling, and was ready to lace the cards, Harold the floorman had acknowledged the fact without even turning his head. 'Two, seven,' Richard told Joe, and then he received a tap on the shoulder, and his replacement arrived, a small Korean girl. The coup was on.

Of course, Richard wasn't there to witness the finale himself, it was relayed to him back at Joe's room, over bottles of champagne and much joy just over an hour later. Everything had gone to plan, just as Richard had said it would. The girl dealt seven winning hands in a row, and the team scooped $24,500. By the time the men in suits arrived, the offset procedure was already under way, and, soon after that, the conspirators slowly peeled away from the table, leaving the poor little Korean girl dealer staring at an empty table with hardly any house chips left. Joe divvied up the money among the team. Richard received his first pay day as a casino cheat, and he now started to wonder what Joe had in mind for their next scam, what Joe was going to teach him and when it was going to happen. He had the buzz. He could hardly wait.

Ten days later, on the way to Joe's flat, he phoned the Four Queens and handed in his notice. When he arrived at Joe's flat, he was about to learn the tricks of the trade that were to make him the best casino cheat in the world. Richard Marcus's new career had begun.

'What would you say,' Joe asked him one day, 'if I told you I could bet $15 on a hand of blackjack, or on a roll of the dice, and get paid a thousand bucks if the bet wins, and only lose the 15 if it doesn't?' He led Richard into his study, where he had a full-sized blackjack table set up. Joe took hold of a stack of red $5 chips from the dealer tray, and placed three in each of the seven betting boxes. 'Go behind the table and deal me seven hands as you would in the casino.'

The shoe on the table was loaded with six decks of cards, just the same as it would have been in a proper casino. Richard dealt Joe the seven hands, and he played each one as any other casino punter would, ensuring he didn't bust. Richard ended up busting, and then Joe told him, 'Pay all the hands exactly as you would in the casino.'

Richard removed a stack of red chips from his tray to pay all the winning hands, and, as he just finished cutting down the three red $5 chips to pay the first box, Joe screamed, 'Hey! That's not right! I'm betting $500 chips here and you're paying me with reds! What's going on here?'

Richard could not believe his eyes. On the first betting post in front of him sat two Tropicana purple chips with a face value of $500 each, capped with a red chip on top of them with a face value of $5. And to make the effect even more dramatic, towards the edge of the table where high rollers keep their valuable chips there was a stack of some more purple chips to complete the illusion. Richard hadn't even noticed him palm the purples on to the table, let alone switch the original bet. Richard was absolutely gobsmacked and was certain any other casino croupier would be too. But he had many questions and reservations as to how this move would pan out in a real casino, with floormen, pit bosses, overhead camera surveillance and of course the possibility of a fellow player on the table grassing on them. Joe set to work to iron out all of Richard's concerns, and explain the move in greater detail. At this stage, as far as Richard was concerned, one thing was certain: the move certainly worked, it was a beauty. It was known in the trade as pastposting, and Richard couldn't wait to get to work on it with Joe and his team in the real environment of a casino, in real life and for real bucks.

The newly formed team practised the move for the rest of the afternoon. Joe explained that the dealer knew in the deep crevices of his brain that the original bet was $15, as most dealers – experienced ones, at least – scan the table carefully before even dealing the cards. But now he sees the $1,005, two purples and a red staring him in the face with the back-up purples on display, all reason and what he has stored in his memory goes completely out of the dealer's head, and he is completely bowled over. And he reaches into his chip tray, fetches out the valuable purple chips and pays, 90-odd per cent of the time. Occasionally, there is heat, and Joe then went on to explain how they had created a sophisticated signalling system between themselves in case they got steam, and had to make a quick exit out of the casino.

Then Joe explained how it worked at the craps table, too. The idea and move was the same, it was just that the method differed somewhat. At craps, as opposed to blackjack, a two-man team was used. The claimer stood behind the mechanic on either end of a busy craps table. The mechanic bet $15, three red chips on the pass-line where players betting with the shooter placed their chips. If the shooter rolled a 7 or an 11 on his first roll, he won. If he rolled a 2, 3 or 12, he lost. Any other number rolled was called a 'point' and had to be rolled a second time before a 7 in order for a pass-line bet to win. If the 7 came out first, pass-line bets lost, and the team were down a mere $15.

If the pass-line bet lost, the mechanic simply bet again after the dealer removed his losing chips. Eventually, the pass-line bet would win, and the mechanic's hand would reach down to the layout as soon as the dealer paid his bet and made the switch, removing the three original red chips and replacing them with two purples and a red. He did this by picking up the three reds with one hand while laying down the move chips with the other, all in a fraction of a second. Then the mechanic yielded his place to the claimer, who immediately put his stack of purple back-up chips in the players' rack along the rail and began claiming that the dealer had paid his bet incorrectly, that he had bet purple chips and only been paid by reds. The cleverness of this move was that the dealer and the boxman (an inspector seated between dealers at either end who watches their payouts and keeps an eye on all the action) had never set eyes on the claimer until that moment. This move was vital, because, if the same person betting $15 on the pass-line for several losing rolls all of a sudden shows up a winner on a thousand-dollar bet nobody has seen him make, the pit would become much more suspicious than if it was evident a new player's thousand-dollar bet was his first bet, plus the valuable purple back-up chips in evidence to back him up as a high roller. It was for this reason – and to keep the pressure on each team member to a minimum – that the team changed who claimed at regular intervals. Joe, of course, was in charge of the security, and would position himself at the end of the craps table, to signal the go-ahead (thumb and index finger on chin), the all-clear to claim the bet (chin) or the quick exit signal (nose) if the heat came on too strong.

Joe decided that Richard was to be the new claimer at the very next game, and gave him this final piece of advice. 'After you have been paid, bet back $205, two black chips with a red on top. That bet makes the original winning bet of the two purples with the red on top look more legit; they will probably think you have a superstition of placing a red chip on top of all your bets. Win or lose, you leave the table after that bet. Sometimes, steam comes after you have been paid, so keep an eye on me and, if I give you the nose, don't even place the bet back, simply say thanks, and leave the table right away. We will have a designated "safe house" to go to where we all meet if there is steam. I will then hang around the table for a little while to see what happens when the pit bosses huddle together, and the suits arrive. They won't know me as I wasn't part of the operation, and would be out of the camera shots from the eye in the sky. Then I'll join you at the rendezvous. All clear?'

That Friday night, Duke, Jerry, Joe and Richard descended on the MGM Grand, where Richard was to claim his first pastpost on a craps table. They found a busy table, with only one boxman, which was a bonus, and were soon in action. Jerry placed his $15 bet, the roller threw a 7, the dealer paid the front-line winners, and in a flash Jerry leaned over and made the switch, turned and walked away. Within a fraction of a second after that, Richard was making his claim, strong and loud. 'Hey, what you doing, man? I'm betting a thousand here, and you're paying me in reds!'

The dealer turned to the boxman, who merely shrugged, and Richard got paid. He then bet the $205 back-up bet, which lost, and then left the table to meet up with the rest of the team in the keno pit, their appointed point of call. Everyone was in awe of Richard's coolness. He had excelled himself on that first go, but the night was still young, and they decided to hit the Dunes as well. There they found another busy craps table with only one boxman, and made a couple more moves, which went like silk. They had cleaned up over three grand on that very first night, and celebrated over a late-night breakfast next to the Dunes. To his delight, Richard realised that this was just the beginning.

After further very successful evenings over the following weeks at blackjack and craps, Joe decided to put Richard in for the next echelon of cheating. Roulette. While the blackjack and craps coups had generated profits at around even money, the attraction of roulette was that winning bets got paid out at a whopping 35 to 1. However, the chip move was far more complicated at roulette, and Joe explained how it was going to work. As Richard was now firmly installed as the new claimer, that would be his job at the roulette. However, this time there was going to be a big difference. At roulette, there is only one croupier, and a floorman who would wander around and be in charge of supervising two tables at once. Any black $100 chips that went into play on roulette had to be announced to the floorman so that a high roller can be monitored. Richard's first move, a very clever psychological one, was to go straight up to the roulette table and place a legitimate bet of $100 on a number. That way, when the team made the move later on the same table, and Richard went to claim, he would already be recognised as a big player. Then the rest of the team would get to work, with a combination of skill, distraction and sleight of hand to end up claiming a pastpost of $100 straight up on a roulette number. The move was audacious and very daring, and extreme skill and split-second timing was essential. The move worked because roulette dealers have to turn their back to the table, only slightly and for just a fraction of a second, after the ball has landed to recover stacks of chips from the back of the table to pay out the winners. It was during this small but very valuable window of opportunity that the team would get to work, and they decided that they were going to go for it at Joe's favourite hotel, the Tropicana, on Saturday evening.

Richard dressed for the part, wearing an expensive suit and borrowing Joe's smart gold watch and diamond ring to portray the image of a high roller. He waltzed up to the roulette table, and placed a $100 black chip on number 4, and the bet lost, so he simply waltzed off again, towards a far-off blackjack table but still close enough to see the signal he was waiting for, a small tug on Joe's right ear. Significantly, however, and exactly as planned, the large bet had been noticed by the dealer who announce to the floorman 'blacks in play', and he eyed up Richard and scribbled a note on his pad.

Richard was now marked as a straight-up, $100-bet-per-number player, and this was to become important in about twenty minutes' time. Now, Jerry and Duke were seated at the same table, having bought dark-blue chips, the farthest ones away from the croupier, and were busy distributing these small-denomination chips all over the green layout, getting ready for Joe's signal by the wheel to put their plan into action. The move was spectacularly simple, yet needed precision timing. As soon as Jerry and Duke received the nod from Joe, Duke bet four of their dark-blue chips on each of the numbers in the third dozen of the roulette wheel – that is, numbers 25 to 36. At the same time, Jerry bet 20 dark-blue chips on the third dozen, 2–1 chance. They repeated this operation until a number in the third dozen actually came up, and the second it did Joe tugged on his ear and Richard was at the table.

'Thirty-three black,' the croupier announced, placing the little plastic dolly on the chips which covered the number and then got to work scooping up all the losing chips off the layout. The side bets were always paid out first on roulette, and, as the croupier turned to reach for the two stacks of blue chips he required, Jerry's hand shot over the table and placed the $100 black chip under the winning chips on number 33. As the croupier turned back to pay the side bet with his two stacks of blue chips, Richard was already congratulating himself. 'Wow! I'm on that, my lucky 33! I love it, what a great casino the Tropicana is. Three-and-a-half grand for my lucky 33!'

The croupier looked at Richard sheepishly. 'I didn't see the black there, I'm gonna have to call over the floorman.'

Charlie the floorman arrived right at the table, and enquired what the problem was.

'He's got a black there, I just didn't see it, boss.'

'Are you sure it was there before the spin?'

'I think so.'

'I'd better call over the pit boss. If you don't mind, sir, this will just take a moment.'

The pit boss wandered over, and the dealer recounted the tale. While he was doing so, Jerry, Duke and Joe were making the table noisy, congratulating Richard on his win, Joe clapping his hands and Jerry telling him to let his bet ride – 'I feel a repetition coming!'

The floorman then delivered what was to save the payout: 'I saw him bet $100 on a number earlier.'

The pit boss nodded to the dealer, who reached for $3,500 worth of black chips, and paid Richard out. He left his $100 bet on for the next spin, and it lost. Richard left the table to join the others at the keno pit, and then they all went off for a drink to celebrate. Richard Marcus's first bet on pastposting roulette had paid off. The roulette road show, which was going to earn them millions, was about to begin. And it was to last for years.

One man went on a crusade to try and stop the party. His name was Steven DeVisser and he worked for Hanson Security, a detective and investigation company employed by many of the major casinos to curb cheating on all the games, to arrest and convict the slot mechanics who were wiring up the machines to pay out jackpots, and also to identify card counters. DeVisser enjoyed a formidable reputation, and had produced results for the casinos, getting many cheats convicted of felonies, and locked up. He knew exactly what Richard Marcus was up to, and did his damnedest to get him pulled, backrooming him many times. But Richard was just too smart for DeVisser, or anyone else for that matter, and was never convicted of any felony – indeed, he only made his astounding story public after his card-playing days were firmly behind him.

All of which makes Richard Marcus, without doubt, the most successful casino cheat in the whole world.

The Flockton Grey Scandal

Mondays have always been a write-off day as far as British horse racing is concerned, allowing overworked and grossly underpaid stable lads a lie-in, trainers the chance to enjoy expensive lunches with wealthy owners in expensive restaurants and hotels, and most yards just ticking over with a reduced staff after a busy weekend, with the quality of racing all over the country being unusually mediocre. It was probably for these very reasons that Ken Richardson chose Monday, 29 March 1982, as the day to pull off one of the largest betting scandals ever to hit British racing.

Ken Richardson was a millionaire Yorkshireman

who had made his fortune from sacks and paper. He was no stranger to making serious money at betting, too, being a massive gambler on horse racing, and a highly successful one, claiming to be winning around £100,000 a year in the late Seventies and early Eighties. He always maintained that money won was much sweeter than money earned, and thoroughly enjoyed beating the bookies at their own game. And he was well armed to do exactly that back then.

Twenty-odd years ago, information provided to the betting public was sparse and manipulated, bookmakers were less wise to coups, and the pricing-up of runners was far less sophisticated than the present-day exchange-driven market. Richardson was also very well organised when it came to placing his bets, and took his task extremely seriously, using a team of about twenty highly trusted associates to place the bets on his behalf. His team included trainers, close friends and business acquaintances who were always sworn to secrecy, and who received a commission for their efforts. Very significantly, Richardson also controlled a string of racehorses in Britain as well as a training operation in Belgium, but he kept his racing and betting affairs complex, and purposely so. It was very difficult to keep track of his horses because he raced them, quite legally, in other people's names and silks. From 1967, his horses ran in his wife Josephine's colours (her very first racehorse, called Rockfire, was trained at Wetherby by Eddie Duffy). By 1970, Mrs Richardson had horses in training with a whole string of trainers, including Eric Collingwood at Malton and Geoff Toft at Beverley. Richardson himself was associated with trainers Pat Rohan, Mick Easterby, Jimmy Etherington, Ken Whitehead, Jock Skilling and Derek Garraton – all with training facilities in the Malton area. He was also well connected with Newmarket trainers Clive Brittain, Pat Haslam, Paul Kelleway, Mick Ryan, Peter Robinson and Brian Lunness. Richardson always made it abundantly clear to his connections and trainers that, as far as he was concerned, the purpose of racing horses was to land gambles, and very substantial ones at that.

In 1973, for example, Brian Lunness trained a two-year-old filly called Jubilee Girl and told Richardson that the horse was probably good enough to win the Brocklesby Stakes at Doncaster, a very valuable early season two-year-old race. Richardson's ears pricked up and his betting mind immediately clicked into gear at the prospect of landing a touch. He instructed Lunness not to enter the filly in the Brocklesby, but to enter her in a much lower-class easier race – the low-grade seller. Richardson figured that, if the trainer considered the horse good enough to win the Brocklesby, it would absolutely walk the seller. He then got to work and backed the horse with £10,000, causing her price to tumble from 4–1 to 13–8. She romped home by seven lengths, landing Richardson another massive pay day from the bookies. Later in the season, however, the trainer was proved right when the horse beat Alexben, the winner of the Brocklesby. How Brian Lunness must have wished he could have run his horses on their merits, and not for money.

But, by 1981, Ken Richardson's racing interests had taken on a sinister agenda. In that year, he purchased a yearling called Flockton Grey for 1,700 guineas. (Bloodstock is always sold in guineas – 1.05 to the pound – even today.) It was an unusual purchase for a shrewd operator like Richardson, as Flockton Grey was an extremely unlikely racecourse star. As a foal, the Dragonara Palace–Misippus colt had changed hands for a mere 900 guineas. Richardson's choice of trainer was strange, too. He sent Flockton Grey to the unfashionable (and not particularly successful) trainer Stephen Wiles at Langley Holmes Stables in Flockton, between Wakefield and Huddersfield.

To complete the scenario, in 1979, another trainer – Colin Tinkler Jr – had bought a horse called Good

Hand as a foal for 600 guineas. This was also an uninspiring purchase and, to make matters worse, a few months after arriving at Tinkler's stable, Good Hand injured his leg on a gate. The injury left a prominent scar on the front of his off-fore leg, just below the knee. Tinkler sold Good Hand to his brother Nigel and, on 22 July 1981, the two-year-old made his debut in a selling race over five furlongs at Catterick. Backed from 5–1 to 2–1 favourite, Good Hand did well to finish third after stumbling out of the starting stalls and completely missing the break. He was third again at Thirsk later that month, and fourth at Ripon in August.

Acting on Ken Richardson's behalf, his right-hand man, Colin Mathison, subsequently claimed Good Hand, which was also a grey and very similar looking to Flockton Grey, for £3,100 and sent him to another training yard, Jubilee Farm. Here, the ownership of the horse changed, as was usual, to one of Richardson's many racing associates, but it was Richardson who supervised and gave the instructions regarding Good Hand – a fact that would become highly significant in the not-too-distant future.

Richardson then entered Flockton Grey into the uninspiring Knighton Auction Stakes for two-year-olds at Leicester on Monday, 29 March 1982. As a debutant from an unremarkable yard, the horse was priced up by the bookmakers at 10–1. Owner Ken Richardson and trainer Stephen Wiles saw an opportunity to make a quick fortune and backed their horse with £20,000, spreading the money around betting shops all over Yorkshire with the use of their trusted contacts in order to avoid detection. Trainer Pat Haslam backed the horse on Richardson's behalf for £250 each way, while Mick Easterby was also on it.

Richardson then arranged for the far better, but similar-looking horse Good Hand to run in place of Flockton Grey. As a three-year-old seasoned ringer, Good Hand was far too strong for the competition, and won by 20 lengths, ridden by Kevin Darley.

This huge margin of victory, particularly for a two-year-old trained by the unfashionable Stephen Wiles, immediately aroused suspicions. Wiles, a former jump jockey, had held a licence for more than two years, yet this was his first success on the flat. Immediately suspecting foul play, the bookmakers refused to pay out. And, to make matters worse, Flockton Grey vanished from Leicester racecourse immediately after the race, preventing a steward's enquiry into him.

The Jockey Club commenced an immediate investigation and sent George Edmondson, an investigator with Racecourse Security Services, to urgently look into the matter. On 31 March, two days after the race, George Edmondson arrived at Langley Holmes Stables. There was a grey two-year-old gelding at the yard and a blood test established with 97 per cent certainty that he was by Dragonara Palace out of Misippus, the breeding of Flockton Grey. But it was not the same horse that had won at Leicester two days earlier. Flockton Grey's passport described a horse with a conspicuous scar on its off-fore leg, below the knee. The grey in Wiles's yard had no such scar. Wiles told Edmondson that Flockton Grey was at Jubilee Farm, 70 miles away at Hutton Cranswick, between Driffield and Beverley, a property owned by Richardson. Not wishing to waste any time, Edmondson drove directly to Jubilee Farm and spoke to Terry Wilson, the manager, but there was no sign of a grey gelding there.

Flockton Grey had vanished. If the winner was not a two-year-old named Flockton Grey, but an older horse, its teeth might have given him away, but no one at Leicester racecourse had examined the winner's teeth. Brian Abraham was the veterinary officer on duty at Leicester, with Pat Morrissey assisting him. Abraham checked the vaccination record in Flockton Grey's passport fleetingly, but not the horse itself. Morrissey checked that some of the horse's markings matched those in its passport but he did not look at its teeth, nor check its off-fore leg for a scar, as Flockton Grey was wearing bandages.

But George Edmondson had a stroke of luck. Ken Bright, the racecourse's official photographer, supplied him with seven pictures of the race. In one, the winner had his mouth open. In young horses, teeth provide a remarkably accurate guide to a horse's age. John Hickman, a veterinary surgeon, and Douglas Witherington, the Jockey Club's chief veterinary officer, examined blown-up photographs of the animal. They were both agreed that, in racing terms, the winner was undoubtedly a three-year-old. Thousands of naming forms and certificates were then examined, in a search for a three-year-old grey with a scar on its off-fore leg, and the investigation homed in on Good Hand.

Richardson's coup had been thwarted and a police investigation commenced. Arrested and pulled in for interview under caution, Richardson claimed he had arranged for Stephen Wiles to take Good Hand away with a view to selling him. Richardson stated that he did not subsequently enquire about the horse, as he was such a busy man, and heard no more of Good Hand until after the Leicester race. According to Richardson, Wiles also bought the Dragonara Palace–Misippus yearling. Peter Boddy, who often drove Richardson's horsebox, delivered the yearling to Wiles early in January 1982.

What could not be disputed, and an element that proved vital in establishing the truth, was a visit paid to Wiles's yard on 5 January 1982 by Philip Dixon, a local veterinary surgeon. Dixon had been asked to complete a naming form for a horse brought to the yard by Boddy, and was handed a foal certificate for a Dragonara Palace–Misippus gelding born on 6 June 1980. The vet did not take the certificate out of its plastic folder, or examine the horse's teeth. He accepted the date of birth on the part of the certificate visible through the plastic and completed the naming form. He entered details of whorls on the horse's head and a scar on the front of the cannon bone on the off-fore leg. The grey was then loaded back into the horsebox, and driven away.

Dixon was to testify in court later, 'I thought it was rather odd that the horse had been brought specifically for me to mark up. I found it fairly odd that it was going straight off again.'

Richardson claimed to know nothing of the horse's subsequent movements. When he had asked Boddy where he had taken the horse, Boddy had replied that he had left it at Wiles's yard, but both Stephen and Elaine Wiles, and stable lad Stephen Pleasant, testified that no horse by the name of Good Hand, or like him, ever appeared at the stable after 5 January. At the end of January 1982, Weatherbys issued a passport for Flockton Grey, bearing the markings of Good Hand but with a date of birth indicating that the horse was a two-year-old. According to Wiles, Mathison subsequently told him to make entries for Flockton Grey. He said that the 'little grey' would be sent to Wiles and, a few weeks before the Leicester race, a little grey duly arrived at his yard.

Wiles testified, 'I did believe it was the horse which I had seen for an hour in the January. I thought it was the horse then named Flockton Grey, and then we started to canter it and found it was absolutely useless, green, nowhere near ready to race, didn't know how to gallop straight, nowhere near fit for entering into a race.'

The trainer looked at Flockton Grey's passport and was reminded of the scar on its off-fore leg. The horse he had been sent, however, did not have a scar. When Wiles phoned Mathison, he was told that Flockton Grey would be with them in time for it to race. Flockton Grey never arrived.

Mathison nevertheless told Wiles to declare the horse for the Leicester race and to book jockey Kevin Darley. Early on the morning of Sunday, 28 March, the day before the race, Boddy arrived and told Wiles he had come for the grey. Later that morning, a horsebox arrived at Geoff Toft's yard at Malton. According to Toft, Richardson had asked him to gallop a two-year-old for him. He had been told that it was a grey. Andrew Harrison, who rode the horse, confirmed Toft's verdict that it was weak and backward and nowhere near ready for racing.

The horse stayed at Toft's until the day after the race – Tuesday, 30 March – when the same driver arrived to take it away. The same day, the grey that had been taken from Wiles on Sunday was returned by Boddy. During the trial, it was put to Richardson that the grey delivered to Toft was the Dragonara Palace-Misippus two-year-old. Richardson denied it. 'That grey was nothing to do with the Wileses,' he said. 'It was a colt belonging to an owner.'

When asked who the owner was, Richardson replied, 'Mr Mel Brittain. I don't expect him to confirm this because he has asked me to keep his name out of it because he is trying to get a licence to train.'

Brittain had horses in training with Peter and Mick Easterby but had ambitions to obtain a licence himself. According to Richardson, Brittain had asked him to arrange for a two-year-old to be tried and Richardson had arranged for it to be tried at Toft's. He was unable to explain why Brittain could not have made the arrangement himself, nor why

Brittain had not used his own horsebox. Brittain was not questioned by the police, nor called to give evidence. Years later, he maintained that Richardson was only a casual acquaintance and that he had not asked him to arrange a trial. It was not Brittain's two-year-old that had been sent to Toft.

On the day of the race, Monday, 29 March 1982, Boddy drove a horse to Leicester racecourse in Richardson's horsebox. According to Boddy, he had picked the horse up from Wiles's yard the previous day as a favour, their horsebox having broken down. That Sunday, he drove the horse to Newmarket, along with another two-year-old grey from Jubilee Farm, which he had to deliver to Pat Haslam's yard. Boddy arrived at Haslam's Pegasus Stables between 6.30pm and 7.30pm. John Hammond, now a leading trainer in France but then Haslam's assistant, was there when the horsebox was opened. Boddy maintained that there were two horses in the box, one intended for Haslam, the other for Leicester, but Hammond testified that there was only one, which he led out himself. 'I don't think I am wrong about this,' he said. 'My clear recollection is there was only one horse in this box when it arrived and that horse was delivered to us and then the box went away.'

Boddy claimed that he had then driven to the nearby Moat House Hotel and parked the horsebox there overnight. If Boddy was telling the truth, the winner of the Leicester race spent about 22 hours standing in the horsebox. At the subsequent trial, Geoffrey Rivlin QC, for the prosecution, accused Boddy of 'lying through his teeth' and described his evidence as 'quite ridiculous and untrue'.

Richardson was also at the Moat House Hotel that evening. He had dinner with Allan Smith, who trained for him in Belgium, and made a number of phone calls, including one to Darley. Richardson advised Flockton Grey's rider that the best piece of ground at Leicester was next to the inside rail. On Monday morning, Boddy left for Leicester, where Wiles had been told to meet the horsebox, with Flockton Grey's passport. Richardson agreed that Ken Haran, a close friend, often placed bets for him but denied that he had asked him to back Flockton Grey.

In a statement to the police, Haran said that he had put substantial bets on for Richardson but, in the witness box, he then retracted his statement. Richardson only accepted responsibility for win bets totalling £1,200 and place bets totalling £850 – very modest sums by his standards. After the race, the winner was loaded into Boddy's horsebox. Wiles expected Flockton Grey to be delivered to his yard, but a grey horse did not arrive until the next day, and then it was the hopelessly backward Dragonara

Palace–Misippus two-year-old. The plot was about to thicken.

Investigators traced Flockton Grey to one of Wiles's yards, determining his identity by blood tests, but found no scar. Good Hand was found later in a remote field in the North York Moors. The case eventually went to trial at York Crown Court in June 1984. Richardson was charged, together with Colin Mathison and horsebox driver Peter Boddy, with conspiracy to defraud. Richardson pleaded not guilty, claiming the mix-up was the trainer's fault, and that nothing had been planned in advance.

The judge, Harry Bennett QC, in summing up the case to the jury, drew attention to the extraordinary nature of the events, stating, 'Members of the jury, I am sure that you must have found in this case, as I have, that it is both curious and fascinating and you may have thought more than once, "Well this would make a very good book, a very good detective story."'

The jury, after a small period of deliberation, were satisfied that the horse in the race was not Flockton Grey but Good Hand, and Richardson was convicted. He was fined £20,000 with £25,000 in costs, and given a suspended nine-month prison sentence. The Jockey Club 'warned off' Richardson for a period of 25 years, and Wiles was banned for the same period. This meant that neither was allowed to attend race meetings, or go onto licensed racing premises. Jockey Kevin Darley, however, was exonerated – it was pointed out that any rider with inside knowledge could easily have held his horse back, making the winning margin seem more respectable and thereby disguising the fraud that had taken place.

Later, Richardson became chairman of Bridlington Town Football Club and 'benefactor' (in his own words) of Doncaster Rovers Football Club. Bridlington Town went bankrupt during his time there, and fans accused the chairman of serious financial misconduct. It was a similar story at Doncaster FC. In 1999, Richardson was convicted of attempted arson, after hiring three men to burn down Doncaster's ground, with a view to collecting insurance money. He received a four-year prison sentence and had to pay costs of £75,000.

In 1996, Richardson's 1984 conviction went to judicial review in the High Court. Expertly represented by Edmund Lawson QC, one of London's most respected barristers, Richardson argued new evidence in his favour. The court, however, would have none of it, and dismissed his appeal. Richardson remained 'warned off' by the Jockey Club, and was ordered to pay £50,000 in costs.

There was another betting coup at Lingfield in

September 1992 in which some allege that it is possible to see links with Richardson, if not direct involvement. A horse won at 33–1. It was bred by the East Riding Sack and Paper Co., a subsidiary of the East Riding Holdings Co. with which Richardson had links and of which he remained the major shareholder from April 1992. It has been said that the same betting shops were used as in the Flockton Grey case.

Ken Richardson now lives on the Isle of Man, but it would not be surprising if he was still involved in the odd gamble or two, despite being 'warned off'.

MIT Students Take On Vegas For Millions

Massachusetts Institute of Technology,
Cambridge, Massachusetts, USA, April 1994

Massachusetts Institute of Technology is one of the most prestigious educational institutions in the United States. Located on 168 acres that extend more than a mile along the Cambridge side of the Charles River Basin, MIT first took on students in 1865 and is steeped in history and culture. Sculptures, murals and paintings are on display throughout the campus, including works by Alexander Calder, Henry Moore, Louise Nevelson, Pablo Picasso and Frank Stella. The main corridors of the central complex feature exhibits on the people who have studied and taught at MIT, many of whom are Nobel Prize winners. MIT excels at sport, too, with more than 65 per cent of all students taking part in intramural sports, and MIT boasts over 1,000 teams, many of whom compete successfully at a very high domestic and international level. After graduation, most students gain employment with elite institutions and companies in finance, consulting, computing or education.

Expected earnings for a graduate with a Bachelor's degree from MIT were around $40,000 a year in 1994. One student in 1994, however, decided that this was way below what he was aspiring to financially, and he had a sport in mind that was not on MIT's published curriculum. He had made up his mind that during the summer vacation he was going to take on Las Vegas, with an unbeatable system that he had discovered and recently perfected. He was going to go to Vegas and take the casinos on at blackjack. Into the bargain, he was going to make the sort of money in a single evening that his contemporaries expected to earn in a year. And not just once, but evening after evening, until he had amassed untold fortunes. And he was going to recruit five students to help him do it.

The road to financial success and glory often

starts with humble beginnings – the brainwave in the bath, the classified advert that produces an avalanche of responses or the spare-bedroom cottage industry that turns itself into a multinational. Simplicity is often the mother of invention, and this incredible story started when, just before the start of the summer recess, a small notice appeared on a bulletin board in the hallway of one of the corridors of Massachusetts Institute of Technology, which simply stated, 'Make Money over the Summer. Play with the MIT Blackjack Team. Saturday morning, April 12. Room 262.'

From this humble beginning – which attracted about forty untidy, unruly and badly dressed students – was born a supremely clever and sophisticated team of geniuses fully trained and prepared to take on Las Vegas for those millions.

Ironically, it was an MIT visiting professor called Edward Thorp who had originally discovered that the game of blackjack was beatable, back in 1963. As blackjack is statistical, and subject to continuous probability, Thorp concluded after a long series of tests and trials that it was a game with a memory, unlike roulette, dice or any other casino game, and that, if a player could remember what had occurred during a game so far, it would give him an insight into what was likely to happen during the rest of the game. This is what is commonly known as 'card counting', although the art of card counting does not actually involve counting cards at all, or remembering which cards have already appeared and in what order. It is quite simply the skill of knowing at any stage in the game how many low cards remain in the deck compared to high cards.

Thorp had stumbled on the fact that when low cards remained in the deck – that is, sevens and lower – the odds were in the house's favour. But, crucially, when there were many high cards remaining (nines, tens, pictures and aces) the odds were in favour of the player. And furthermore, given that casinos use six decks in blackjack, the further into these decks that the count is high, the better the advantage to the player.

The team leader student at this first meeting of MIT applicants had already learned, practised and memorised Thorp's theories. From hours and hours of practice most evenings at the back of the library, he had also learned how to keep the mental count through the entire six decks of cards, by awarding a value of plus one for all cards two to six, and a value of minus one for all tens, pictures and aces. He soon also came to appreciate that sevens, eights and nines were considered non-runners, or dead cards, and he did not factor them into the equation. Therefore, by keeping a running total in his head of the cards that had been dealt, a high positive count would mean that a lot of low cards had already been dealt, and the deck was rich in high cards, and a high negative count would mean that a lot of high cards had come out and there were a lot of low cards left in the deck. This was the golden key to unlocking the secret of blackjack, a secret that could give the player the impossible – the ultimate edge over the house – and at the same time reap enormous financial rewards. And that was, quite simply, the basis of the formula used by the select few, the super-clever card counters who were held in awe by their peers in casinos and gaming clubs all over the world.

Of course, in real life it wasn't going to be that simple. Quite a few card counters had already mastered this system, and won some money – upon which the house would get wise to their play fairly quickly and simply ask them to leave and not to return. Casinos are not charities, and they are aware of their Achilles heel at blackjack. The telltale sign is a player who sits patiently for hours, playing the minimum bet, and suddenly ups the ante to the table maximum when the count is in his favour, and then immediately reduces it again after the successful run is over. Such players, although they picked up decent sums of money in the meantime, were quickly tumbled and excluded from their clubs. And casino security were eager to swap their information, together with profiles and mugshots of card counters, with their opposite numbers, so that known counters couldn't play in a game – not only in their home towns, but anywhere in the world. The American casinos even went to the lengths of hiring exclusive and expensive private detective agencies to track and monitor cheats, thieves and card counters to protect their bankrolls.

Through the use of sophisticated surveillance cameras, the agencies produce digitally enhanced photos in books of everyone who has ever been evicted from a casino. Furthermore, some of the agencies even went to the lengths of gathering personal information about the culprits, including home addresses and telephone numbers. Despite this obstacle, the MIT student was supremely confident of success, and quite rightly so. After all, there were quite a few factors that tilted the odds in his favour. First, age – most established card counters were single males in their thirties and forties, some even older. A group of students, posing as rich kids, would most likely blend into a casino background without raising too much suspicion. Second, sex. He was not aware of any female card counters, certainly not any who had been caught to date. And thirdly, and most importantly, he had devised methods to vastly improve and capitalise on Thorp's original basic strategy. This mathematical genius had massaged, tweaked and caressed Thorp's theory to the ultimate. All he needed now was a reliable team, and he was determined, at this initial meeting in room 262, to start putting his team together.

As well as improving the actual count itself, he had decided that he would have teams of players in the casinos hovering around and playing on different tables all at once, in order to up the ante and max out on their potential, as well as spotters on the tables and in the crowds who would do the counting for the players and discreetly signal to the players when the count was in their favour. This was going to be run like a military operation, and he immediately got to work at this first meeting to see who had the potential to pass the tests and fulfil his dreams and ambitions.

The team leader stood up to address the group. He was barely five foot four with slicked-back hair and bushy eyebrows. He wore designer jeans, a flashy silk shirt and loafers. His name was Andre Martinez, and his reputation preceded him. He was an absolute genius, to the point that the maths professors had fast-tracked him to graduate-level seminars after only three days on campus. Martinez spoke softly, but with purpose. 'I have found a method, which I have perfected myself, to make fortunes playing blackjack in Las Vegas. For the past 18 months I have devoted every single evening to fine-tuning this system both here and at casinos in Las Vegas and Atlantic City most weekends. Along the way I have accumulated over £400,000 in cash, sufficient for our stake money to take our play to the next, higher level of reward. A level each and any one of you can be involved in. And I can promise you this: when we have selected our team of six from you guys, you will earn money beyond your wildest dreams. More than you could ever imagine.'

The room had now fallen completely silent. To make the MIT team, the students had to pass three tests with flying colours. When Edward Thorp had discovered card counting way back in 1963, it had been used by single lonely guys playing in casinos on their own. They made money, but were quickly spotted and barred from all the casinos. The idea of playing as a team had never been considered before. The team was to be split into three groups: spotters, gorillas and big players, each with their own individual role, each as important as the other, and each with the potential to earn themselves an absolute fortune.

Martinez now had his audience in his grasp.

Spotters, he explained, are part of the team who sit at the blackjack tables and play for the minimum bet available, just like every other mug, tourist and small-time punter at the blackjack tables all over the world – sometimes winning a little, sometimes losing a little, but never changing their stake and eventually surrendering their hard-earned dollars to the house. 'The difference is,' he went on, 'that when our guys play they are also doing the count. The second the count goes favourable, the spotter signals a gorilla or big player, who immediately moves in on the table. A gorilla is a player who bets big. Now, the second he hits the table, he has to pretend to be some rich-kid big-hitter, probably drunk, and throwing his money all over the place. In reality, he is just betting good hand after good hand, doesn't do any counting and simply waits until the spotter signals that the good run of cards is over. He simply then gets up and roams the casino floor awaiting his next call-up from another spotter.

'A big player,' Martinez continued, trying his best to sound matter-of-fact and running his hand through his hair, 'is what I have perfected over this past year and a half. I act, I count and I bet. I have even perfected monitoring the shuffle, previously thought an impossible feat. When dealers are shuffling the cards, it is dead time for the casino, as they are not making any money. Many dealers have been encouraged to shuffle lightly and quickly so as not to waste valuable betting time. I have perfected a technique where I can follow and track the shuffle, and even cut the deck to an ace, giving me a massive advantage over the house.'

Cutting to the ace, he went on to explain, was a sophisticated move whereby a very experienced big player sometimes caught a glimpse of an ace during the shuffle, could cut the deck to a predetermined number of cards and then know precisely when the ace was about to appear. Naturally, a large wager would await the arrival of the prized card. A big player has the most onerous of tasks – he becomes known to the casino very quickly and receives lots of privileges, such as free luxury suites and food, because he is betting regularly with thousands of dollars. So that is where the acting comes in: you have to play casually enough not to alert the casino to what you are really up to.

'I am quite convinced that the bulk of you here are able to pass these tests.' The audience were now sitting open-mouthed in awe at what they had heard. 'If any of you feel this is not for you, or that your studies will be at risk, please leave the room now.'

Six students shuffled out, the rest remained.

Martinez then dropped his bombshell. 'We have all

heard the stories about the lengths casinos used to go to to frighten off winners. The beatings in dark casino basements by armed security thugs. Hotel rooms and safes being broken into and winnings confiscated. Even the long drives into the desert from which you did not return. That was in the days of the mob rule of Vegas over twenty-five or thirty years ago. All that has changed now. The casinos are now owned by multinationals such as Hilton, and, while they will go to extreme lengths to protect their golden chest, I can promise you the team will not be at risk from any violence. We might well experience intimidation, barring and even the invitation to attend the casino security manager's windowless offices in the casino basements. But they won't harm us, guaranteed. And they won't confiscate our winnings. Promise. Everyone still interested?'

The 35 glanced at each other but no one else left the room. Out of the 35 that remained, the MIT team was to be selected.

Within a couple of weeks, Martinez had made his selection, and nine hours a day, seven days a week, the team practised the count, followed by the spotting and gorilla tests. They were taught to self-deal six decks of cards, and master the techniques. Many took decks of cards back to their rooms and dealt themselves hands into the early hours of the morning. The brightest of the group went on for extra training in the art of following the shuffle, cutting the deck to predetermined numbers of cards and acting the part. This was an intense crash course in beating blackjack, and over the coming weeks during that long hazy summer recess of 1994 Martinez became more and more excited and satisfied with the results. Finally, by August, they had perfected their act and the team were fully prepared. The MIT blackjack card-counting team, the carefully selected team of six, were ready. And they were heading for Las Vegas.

Tropicana Casino, Atlantic City, June 1993

For about 18 months prior to the inaugural meeting in room 262 in April 1994, the original MIT group of one, Martinez, masqueraded as a tourist (usually with a friend in tow) most weekends in Atlantic City. Famous for its Broadwalk, originally built in 1870 to stop the sand blowing into the hotel foyers, and the most expensive property you can own in Monopoly, since the late Seventies Atlantic City had become the playground for North American gamblers. Elegant casinos sprang up in five-star beachfront hotels, offering their guests gourmet dining, spas and pampering, indoor and outdoor pools, revue shows and headline entertainment. The casinos themselves boasted the latest slots, roulette, craps, poker and, of course, blackjack. Taking turns in pairs, they took on different casinos every weekend, often checking in with an alias, for obvious reasons. The IT and internet boom was just starting, and the casinos were very happy to welcome and entertain rich kids whom they assumed were doing well in the infancy of the technology boom. Nothing could have been further from the truth as far as Martinez and his guests were concerned. They were using these weekends to put their systems to the test – with awesome results. This weekend it was Martinez's turn to introduce Kevin Lewis to real-life blackjack for the first time. And it was Lewis's job to walk through the airports and avoid Customs with $40,000 in hundred-dollar bills, their stake money, strapped to his torso with masking tape.

The limousine was waiting for them at Newark airport. The Tropicana host sprung out of the rear passenger door and greeted Martinez. Turning to Kevin, he shook his hand. 'I'm Dino Taratolli, I'm Mr Kim's host at the Tropicana. Welcome to our hotel.'

The two boys slid into the cool leather interior of the limo nimbly followed by Dino the host, and they sped off towards the resort.

On the journey Kevin couldn't help but strike up a

chat with Dino. 'What does a host do exactly?' he enquired innocently.

'Well, son, as Mr Kim has found out to his benefit over the past few months, my job is to look after the big players. As soon as we see you play for thousands, we offer you the works, to keep you coming back, and to stop you straying to our competitors. That's why I have reserved you both a fabulous suite, with complimentary champagne and food. I am available for you guys to make your stay as comfortable as possible. Anything you need, and I mean anything, don't hesitate.'

Kevin's mind was now working overtime. He had visions of a suite full of scantily clad beauties with lines of charlie in the bathroom and buckets of champagne by the Jacuzzi. Martinez was attending to his second vodka from the limo's mini bar, when they pulled into the long drive leading up to the Tropicana entrance. Five minutes later, Dino having ensured they bypassed the formalities of reception check-in, they were alone in a sumptuous suite, complete with two bedrooms, two bathrooms, a bar and a living room with a circular leather couch and 40-inch plasma-screen TV. 'Wow!' was all Kevin could say as he reached under his shirt and peeled off the wads of hundred-dollar bills. 'Tell me, what's with all this Mr Kim business?'

Martinez laughed. 'Did I forget to tell you? I'm known as Robert Kim here. Let's freshen up, and hit the tables.'

Twenty minutes later, they were heading towards the high-stakes blackjack tables, in a quiet corner of the casino, past the forest of slots, roulette tables, keno and small games of blackjack, all busily in action with tourists in shorts and T-shirts off the Broadwalk, and a few better-dressed businessmen from Manhattan taking the weekend off. The MIT two each had $20,000 in notes in their pockets, ready for Kevin's first taste of playing the game for real money.

Martinez chose an empty table with a smart and quite stunning Korean croupier in attendance. The decks of cards were fanned out over the green baize, all six decks, all in order. A little plastic sign indicated that the minimum bet was $100, and the maximum $5,000. Martinez sat at the end chair on the left, and Kevin sat next to him, his heart pounding. The dealer started shuffling the cards, Martinez peeled off $5,000 in cash to change up for chips, and Kevin, as per instructions, did the same. The dealer offered the cards to be cut, and then placed them in the shoe to be dealt. She then counted two-and-a-half stacks of black $100-dollar chips for each player. There was very little in it for either of them for the bulk of the hands, Kevin sticking to a hundred a hand while Martinez oscillated between a hundred and three. Then, quite suddenly, with only half a dozen or so hands left to go until the end of the shoe, Martinez suddenly bet $1,000. Kevin upped his ante to $500. The dealer dealt them both queens, and herself a five. Kevin's next card was the ace of hearts, winning him $750, while Martinez's was another queen. Martinez, against all casino etiquette, split the queens, receiving a face card on each, and then the dealer drew a nine followed by a ten to bust. They had just won $4,750 on that one hand alone. The next few hands went the same way, and by the end of the shoe they were up well over ten grand between them. After colouring up their chips into higher-value ones and stuffing them in their pockets, Martinez grabbed Kevin by the wrist and literally dragged him from the table, straight to the bar for large ones.

Kevin stared at Martinez in awe. 'Christ, that was unreal. Ten grand. In ten minutes. I don't believe it.'

'Wait till you see what we do with a team, Kevin. *That* you won't believe, I promise you. It will be much bigger, very much bigger,' Martinez assured his new team-mate as they downed their drinks and headed to the next unsuspecting blackjack table to run up their profits, ahead of the big one. Martinez simply couldn't wait.

MGM Grand Casino, Las Vegas, November 1994

Martinez had booked three suites at the MGM Grand for three of the team leaders on a Thursday, all under the name of Peter Koy, president of a software company in Silicon Valley. The rest of the team were instructed to arrive at different times on the following day, and to sign in under agreed false names into the Stardust. The entire team held in their possession false Californian driving licences with their photos on, all of which had been uplifted from their MIT yearbook – a decision that, in the fullness of time, they would come to regret. They were all to be in the casino at the stroke of midnight on the Friday evening to start work, at predetermined tables. They were also told that they shouldn't been seen together in groups too frequently, as the MGM complex had installed thousands of cameras. Some of these were cleverly concealed behind false ceilings, others in the lighting, and they were switched around every few days to confuse the punters and to prevent cheats keeping track of them. Furthermore, there were cameras in the hotel corridors, elevators, foyers and even some leading into the washrooms. It was imperative that security didn't latch on to them as a group. They had been briefed: 'Whenever we are in public, make out we don't know each other. Use the names we have agreed, never your real ones, and, if you need a break, or need to go back to your room, make sure you go on your own. And no need to bother with ordering those soppy energy drinks – all the casinos in Vegas have high levels of oxygen pumped into their ventilation systems to keep punters awake longer.'

By five o'clock the following afternoon, everyone had arrived as planned, and the hours were ticking away to the midnight commencement of action. At the Stardust, Kianna (the only female member of the team) removed $100,000 from plastic bags that had been strapped with masking tape to her thighs for the flight from beneath her clothes in the bathroom. She was quite a beautiful girl, with pouting lips and shapely legs, and had been encouraged to dress the part for the casino, in the hope of getting chatted up by male players on the tables in order to help disguise her role.

On another floor of the Stardust, Fisher, a mathematics master, undid his money belt, also containing $100,000. The third member of the team at the Stardust was Mickey, a preppy tennis jock, while Brian, a physics geek, completed the trio at the MGM.

Back at the MGM, Kevin and Martinez sat in their respective suites dealing themselves cards for the umpteenth time before the real run. Kevin, even though he was the one who had practice from Atlantic City, was particularly nervous, like an actor who had learned his lines thoroughly and been word perfect for countless rehearsals, yet insisted to himself on checking them over word for word in his dressing room on opening night.

At midnight, the predetermined time, Martinez, Kianna, Kevin, Fisher, Brian and Mickey were seated at four blackjack tables in the high rollers, minimum $100, maximum $5,000 stake tables at the MGM. Martinez was wearing a purple velvet shirt with gold medallion, black leather trousers and with his gelled slicked-back hair seemed the epitome of a rich kid in the pop business. His counter was Kianna, who looked stunning in a low-cut dress, heavy make-up and heels. She was certainly very well disguised as a spotter. Kevin, the other big player, was seated five tables away with Mickey counting, and on the third and fourth tables Fisher and Brian sat playing the minimum and keeping a continuous count. All carried huge wads of cash in hundred-dollar bills and their fake Californian driving licences.

At Martinez's table, nothing had happened for the first two shoes, the count never going over positive three, and staying mostly below zero for the two shoes. Suddenly, on Fisher's table, an opportunity was developing. A beautifully cut shoe, over five decks deep, had just been inserted into the dealing shoe, providing a magnificent counting opportunity. The first few hands were rich in twos, threes and fours, the count shot up to 15, and it was time to pounce. Brian wandered over to Martinez and gave the signal, and in time for the next deal Martinez was seated next to Fisher. No one could have guessed that they even knew each other. Martinez played the part of the drunk rich kid superbly, sipping on his second vodka and tonic and throwing his chips into the betting circle nonchalantly. The cards were coming out: Fisher got a ten, and Martinez a queen. The dealer received a five, and Fisher matched his ten with a nine, while Martinez received another queen. He had $1,400 in the box, and he chose to split the queens, normally a dreadful decision, but in these circumstances a fabulous play with the odds massively in his favour. The croupier tilted his head slightly to the pit boss behind him and uttered 'splitting tens'. The pit boss looked over at the velvet shirt and just nodded. Out came the cards, an ace and a ten. Bingo! The dealer dealt himself a nine followed by a jack and bust. The whole table won, Martinez cleaning up three and a half grand in just that one hand alone. By 3am, the team had made that figure tenfold, and left almost as unnoticed as they had arrived, nearly forty grand up.

The following day, they did it again: this time, sixty grand. Then they started moving from casino to casino, winning regularly well into five figures between them every session. They hit the million mark with three weeks to go until Christmas. The team decided to go for the chandeliers in the run-up to Thanksgiving – they felt the casinos would be off-guard at that busy time, and they were determined to max out on their potential. And they weren't disappointed. By Christmas Eve, they were up to three million and, through great acumen and clever agility around the Vegas scene, had got away with their coup undetected.

In 1995, the team grew to 12. They were now slicker than ever, donning disguises, changing their names and casinos regularly, and continued to clock up their profits. But the casinos were now conscious that something was amiss. The wins had become large enough to be noticed, and the team's run had been noted by various casino security departments, who by now were employing private detective agencies to monitor play and also to share information with each other to wipe out the cheats. Although card counting was not cheating as such, and a case against it wouldn't stand up in court, the

PI agencies were just as keen to get the photo IDs of counters in their books alongside the cheats and went to great lengths to discover who they were.

One man on a mission against the cheats and counters was Vincent Cole of Plymouth Security. He had a formidable reputation. He had once caught an Australian card counter, and taken him downstairs. After photographing him, and making him sign the trespass form barring himself for life from the casino, he had told the two security guards to leave them alone in the room. He then pulled a gun on the Aussie, asking him how much he had won over the past year. The poor kid was too scared to speak. Cole then produced a purple $500 chip. 'You've eaten quite a lot of these here over the past twelve months, but this is the one you are going to remember.' He then made the wretched Australian swallow the chip. The thing got stuck in his throat, and he turned as purple as the chip. He very nearly choked to death right there. Somehow he got it down, but he never counted cards again.

Cole simply adored watching the videos of high-stakes players from the casino surveillance rooms, and was constantly checking and cross-referencing players from one casino to the other – especially those who were winners at blackjack. By May 1995, he was convinced there was a team of sophisticated counters at work, a team who had amassed millions courtesy of the MGM, Caesar's, Mohegan's and any other casino that would accommodate them. And these were casinos who, in their greed, had comped these players with free suites, meals, gifts and booze in a vain attempt to recoup their losses.

Cole wanted them, and he wanted them bad. If they were a team, and had gone about their business unnoticed, they must know each other from somewhere. But where? Then it suddenly dawned on him. They were college kids, they knew each other from school or university. They had probably practised all summer holiday, for Christ's sake. He ordered every college yearbook he could think of, and then went through every photo meticulously. And there they were, all six of them together, in the MIT yearbook for 1993. Cole smiled to himself as he slowly closed the book.

It took two months for the team to be formally tumbled, and it was at Mohegan's that they met their Waterloo. Martinez was disguised as a Japanese businessman and they were playing as usual when he noticed three men in suits walk towards the blackjack area. They huddled around something, and Martinez decided to go and look. It was a fax machine, and it was spluttering out pages of printed information, followed by pages of photos. Out of the corner of his eye, he saw the insignia of Plymouth Security at the top of one of the pages. And the photos were of him. The suits were on mobile phones now.

In a flash he remembered what he had taught himself all that time ago, when it first began: 'Remember when the time is right to walk away.' And walk they did, with over $10 million of casino money in total. They'd got out just in time. It was only much later that one member of the team spilled the beans on the amazing escapade.

The golden age of card counting is now virtually over, with the casinos having wised up and installed continuous shuffling machines. But you might still find the odd one with the old-fashioned dealer's shoe, and, if you do, keep your eyes open. Who knows, you might find an old-fashioned card counter at work there too.

5

The SkyBiz Multi-Million-Dollar Internet Scam

While most of the scams and gambles detailed in this book have happened live, person to person, in the real world – face to face, so to speak – the internet has opened up a whole new world of opportunity for scammers intent on making a fast illegal buck. And it has given them the opportunity to achieve their aims worldwide, with millions of potential victims to target at a very low overhead cost, thanks to the wonders of cyberspace. In the late 1990s, one man thought up a scheme so audacious, but so breathtakingly simple, that it was to take the financial world in cyberspace by storm, and raise millions of dollars for the founders of the plan, while leaving the bulk of investors penniless.

The brains behind this scam was a man called James Brown, a veteran wallet-thinner of audacious nerve and dubious background. His partner in crime was a man named Elias Masso (it is not clear whether they had been in business together before this venture, but most likely they had). Brown came up with an idea that was simple, but one that he felt sure would work. He was going to pyramid scheme the idea of selling websites on the internet to the general public. On the basis that everybody would love to own their own website, he decided to go ahead with the venture and formed a company called SkyBiz.com Inc. Of course, it wasn't the websites itself that held the attraction of quick riches for Brown, it was the potential of the gullible public marketing the idea to each other, selling the story and recruiting new members. Otherwise known as multi-level marketing, or the classic pyramid scheme.

Brown moved quickly and approached another company called 'World Service Corporation' to peddle his idea and they were delighted to assist him – for a large fee, of course. Brown appointed them to perform the back-room functions for SkyBiz, which included the construction of a token website for illustration on the internet, bulk-emailing and the handling of incoming emails and memberships. But one could be forgiven for thinking that the response, and the speed in which the money rolled in, took even Mr Brown, his partners and his cronies at World Service Corporation by surprise. The idea flew from day one.

Most people, apart from the very young, have received a chain letter at some time in their lives. It preys upon the common human desire to get something for nothing, and the logic is simple – send away a few dollars for a few names and wait for the money to roll in. 'Chain' isn't really the right word for this well-used scam, though – the correct term should be 'pyramid'. Many pyramid schemes have been created over the years, but each one has a common denominator. A small number of 'Sharks' in the upper levels are given money by a much larger number of 'Fish' underneath. The Fish hope that the pyramid will keep expanding downwards, with new and bigger levels of Fish, so that they will graduate to being Sharks in the upper section of a bigger pyramid. These schemes cannot possibly last for ever, and they are now illegal. To be legal, the scheme would have to actually offer its members something for their money, not just the promise of large returns. However, Brown reasoned, quite cleverly, that, as SkyBiz was offering a website within the scheme, that would make the whole thing legal – or at least take the heat off the situation for sufficient time to get the money rolling in.

The reason these pyramid schemes are illegal is simple: the world does not contain an infinite supply of new Fish. All these pyramid schemes are destined to fail almost as soon as they are launched, because they assume that more and more people will join them, and eventually the scheme becomes saturated, and the Fish at the bottom end lose out, while the few Sharks (usually only 1 per cent of the total membership) coin it in. In the Information Era, the internet makes many things easier, including separating Fish from their money. Every day, countless variations of the chain letter are sent in their millions by email to all corners of the world. Pyramid schemes, now called 'network selling' or 'multi-level marketing', promise great wealth in exchange for a small investment and recruitment of a few new members. SkyBiz was one of the most intriguing of these, selling not household items, cosmetics or vitamins, but websites. 'Every family needs one,' says the blurb in the lavishly printed brochures with photos of the President and CEO James Brown smiling at his public. No one seemed to care one iota that most people connected to the internet have already been offered a free website by their service provider and less than 10 per cent have taken up the offer. That kind of negativity was cleverly overlooked by the promoters of this scheme, when peddling the road of promised riches to their customers. With SkyBiz, the attraction was not the website itself, but the wealth that would follow from setting up your home business promoting the scheme to new levels of Fish – and, of course, most handsomely lining the pockets of the promoters behind it.

Word spread like wildfire, and SkyBiz was soon flavour of the month. Emails were excitedly exchanged over cyberspace and the new idea was the hot topic of conversation in pubs, bars and offices all over the world, in factories, at dinner parties, amongst excited gatherings of young entrepreneurs and in City boardrooms. But the word spread to the authorities quickly, too, and as with all other bubbles – the South Sea Company, Dutch tulips, Poseidon and Polly Peck – the authorities stepped in rapidly to spoil the party. The courts quickly ordered a Temporary Receiver to be appointed to take control of SkyBiz's affairs.

Once the Receiver was appointed to SkyBiz.com, the full extent of the fraud was soon revealed. The Receiver discontinued sales with immediate effect, took control of the company's corporate bank accounts and dismissed the bulk of the staff who were employed by the company. Documents and computer files were seized, as were the company's financial ledgers. And the net soon widened. It was discovered that SkyBiz.com had an office in Australia with ten employees, although that office did not accept orders for products or sign up new members – it was just part of an elaborate audit trail that had been cleverly constructed by Brown to put the authorities off the scent. Another office was discovered in Birmingham, Alabama, which was used by World Service Corporation to prepare the SkyBiz newsletters and training manuals. By painstakingly ploughing through the haystack, the Receivers soon found the needles they were searching for, including further offshore entities and bank accounts. One such company was SkyBiz International (Bermuda) Ltd, K.F.B.B. and Masso Limited. These companies operated under common ownership, enjoyed substantial inter-company benefits, and were used to disguise substantial funds that had been redirected by Brown. Some of these huge sums had been used to invest in real estate and provide inter-company loans for trading with, and yet another corporation, Nanci, had control of a credit-card merchant account that had put through millions of dollars of victims' credit-card payments.

But it was when the Receiver took control of the Company's bank accounts that they found the holy grail they were looking for, and a massive financial asset. They discovered an account at Merrill Lynch in Bermuda in the name of SkyBiz International Ltd that had an account balance of $28.4 million. Further assets were soon uncovered in Mexico, Texas and other exotic locations. These had been cleverly hidden as wire transfers, but were, in reality, assets in the form of properties. Further assets were uncovered at the Bank of Butterfield in Bermuda and in the British Virgin Islands. Attempts had also been made to hide money at Bank Hapoalim in Israel, but had failed. Some requests by the Receivers to track further hidden assets failed, however, as certain banks refused to co-operate as they were outside the jurisdiction of the American courts. All in all, SkyBiz had pulled in over $37 million dollars from its hapless victims over an astonishingly short period of time, although a few million, as with most famous fraud cases, remained unaccounted for. By the time the court-appointed Receiver had finished his work, it became evident that the number of Fish who had enjoyed any sort of commission rebate from SkyBiz amounted to less than 1 per cent, with over 96 per cent of SkyBiz's customers losing money. The Sharks had milked the system dry.

In May 2001, the directors of SkyBiz were filed with a suit charging them with promoting a pyramid scheme. The money located by the Receiver was used to compensate victims and became part of the settlement between the scheme's promoters and the Federal Trade Commission. The promoters were also barred from participating in promoting any further pyramid operations. They were extremely lucky not to go to prison. SkyBiz was a fabulous gamble while it lasted, but it was destined to fail from the beginning, as all pyramid schemes ultimately do.

The Malaysian Football
Betting Scam

In the last two decades, Malaysia has undergone tremendous growth and prosperity. Many attribute the country's success to the dynamic leadership of Prime Minister Mahathir bin Mohammed, who has led the country since 1981. During this period of financial prosperity, stability and growth, many Malaysians have developed a keen interest in betting on sport, especially English Premier League football. Although betting in Malaysia is, strictly speaking, illegal, many black-market bookmakers have sprung up over the past twenty years, and given the huge amount of interest and cash flowing in their direction, many of these bookmakers have become financially very powerful and astute, to the point that, today, Malaysia finds itself home to some of the biggest football bets, struck from well-connected punters and bookmakers all over the world.

Sometimes, profitable arbitrage situations arise in which the Malaysians, in order to balance their books, are offering a price on a match that, quite simply, can lock in a profit for an astute punter if he is prepared to 'arb' the other two sides of the transaction with his bookmakers at home. Although the profit is sometimes as little as 1 per cent, many big operators are quite happy to make this turn on the outcome of a football game, and it is these betting propositions that keep the Malaysians at the forefront of the betting arena. The illegal underground Malaysian bookmakers command huge trust and respect from their counterparties worldwide, even today. And it was in Malaysia that the concept of Asian Handicap betting on English football was conceived just a few years ago, a concept that was to take the world of football betting by storm, dominate the betting industry with millions of pounds' worth of bets per match ante post and in running, and result in one of the biggest betting scams ever to hit the English Premiership.

'In-running' betting is a concept where

bookmakers make a price on an event after it has commenced, and will continue to make a price until the result. The potential is quite phenomenal. Imagine a home team, odds-on favourites, going one–nil down after a few minutes of play. Now a new market will be formed, with the home team's price having expanded, and that of the away team shortening. Should an equaliser be scored with minutes to go until the final whistle, the draw becomes favourite, and so on. On the betting exchange Betfair, betting in running on a Premiership football game frequently attracts hundreds of thousands of pounds' worth of bets.

The concept of Asian Handicaps on football betting, however, needs to be understood fully to appreciate the planning that goes on behind the scenes in order to pull off these audacious betting coups. As well as the normal 90-minute odds on a match, and the in-running markets quoted by the likes of Ladbrokes, Coral and William Hill in every high street every weekend, an Asian Handicap is created by bookmakers that gives a roughly equal chance to both teams. This is achieved by awarding the underdogs a head start in goals, or a handicap. This allows a very competitive market to be offered to the customer, even if the match is a very one-sided affair with a strong favourite. Although Asian

Handicaps may appear complicated at first, and have various permutations to them, they are actually very easy to understand, and the shrewd punters in the Far East were quick to pick up on this new and exciting concept. So too were a team of scammers and Asian criminals, who spotted a window of opportunity in the structure of Asian Handicap betting on football – a window of opportunity they were very keen to exploit at all costs, with a potential return of many millions of pounds.

The criminal fraternity involved in football betting scams in Malaysia had suddenly been forced to change their modus operandi. Up until the mid-1990s, football matches in Malaysia were blatantly rigged, but, when more than 100 players and officials were arrested for corruption, it persuaded the criminal elements to ignore the Malaysian fixture list, and it made the British Premiership an obvious target for the corrupt betting syndicates that preyed on the popularity of gambling in the Far East. Furthermore, after the unwelcome publicity accompanying the acquittal of Bruce Grobbelaar, Hans Segers and John Fashanu on match-fixing charges in 1997, the gangs shifted their efforts to technical sabotage, rather than their original method of trying to bribe players and officials.

The advent of Asian Handicap betting on English

Premiership football matches opened the door for these corrupt betting syndicates to rig matches, without going to the trouble of bribing players or officials. The complex betting scam worked because the rules that were applied by bookmakers to punters betting on Asian Handicaps were flawed. As the betting worked principally around encounters between the largest and smallest clubs in the Premier League, the handicap awarded to the underdogs in Asian Handicap betting would frequently be one or two goals in their favour. So, for example, in a hypothetical Arsenal vs. Wimbledon game, the Wimbledon side would be given a two-goal start, or handicap. In the Far East, millions would still be wagered on Arsenal, at slightly odds-on, despite the handicap advantage handed to Wimbledon. This meant, in a nutshell, that Arsenal had to overcome the disadvantage and win the match by more than two goals, and, if they did so, punters would be paid out at far more attractive odds than if they had bet on Arsenal outright at deep odds-on. The corrupt betting syndicates figured that, if Wimbledon were still ahead by the start of the second half, and they could find a way to – say – kill the floodlights at the ground, causing the match to be abandoned, under the Asian Handicap betting rules, the result, and the bets made on it, stood.

This was because the Asian betting market had different rules to the UK market. Whereas bookmakers in the UK only paid out if the match was completed and the full ninety minutes played, in the Far East bets were settled if the match passed half-time, even if it was abandoned. All the syndicates needed were some accomplices in the UK prepared to take the risk and bribe employees to help them on their way at the football stadiums themselves. By 1996, the hunt for such accomplices was firmly on, bankrolled by the largest and most crooked of the Malaysian betting cartels.

London thrives on Far-Eastern business, and in Soho's Chinatown betting is rife; bookmakers have sprung up on almost every street corner. Illegal gambling dens are frequented until the early hours of the morning, and the Chinese are regular visitors to West End and suburban casinos, where it is not uncommon to hear a noisy roulette table buzzing with Chinese voices. Freeholds of Chinese restaurants themselves have changed hands during rapid, noisy and passionate games of Mah Jong in back rooms in Soho, or the turn of a card in grotty basements. Illegal Far-Eastern immigrants were taken on to work for pittances as slave labour, lining the pockets of the Chinese restaurateurs, many of whom had ties to the Chinese underworld. This was exactly the environment from which the Malaysians were looking to recruit their soldiers, and they put the word out in London that they were looking for operators for their scheme, accomplices who would be very well rewarded indeed for the risks they were prepared to take on board. The Malaysians didn't have long to wait for their eager applicants to pop up, delighted and intrigued that the well-tested Chinese grapevine had once again got to work efficiently.

Wai Yuen Liu was born in Hong Kong but had lived in London for a number of years and held a British passport. He was a very heavy gambler, like most of his Chinese friends, and had been a member of the Golden Horseshoe Casino in West London since 1994. He visited that casino almost every evening over a two-year period, and during that time had lost about £120,000. This was an absolute fortune for a man who was claiming benefits and living in a council flat, and who worked part-time as a washer-up in a Chinese restaurant in Soho. He was heavily in debt to credit-card companies and many banks, as well as the impatient and violent Chinese moneylenders. As a gambler under pressure for funds, and thirsty for fresh financing, Liu was an ideal target for the Malaysian betting syndicate, and they had no hesitation in making contact with him. Coincidentally, he had two friends, Chee Kew Ong and Eng Hwa Lim, who would also turn out to be useful contacts for the paymasters in Malaysia – especially Lim, who was an electronics engineer. The betting cartel in Malaysia, keen to move without any delay, summoned the trio for an urgent meeting.

On a crisp evening in September 1997, the Malaysians sent a Jaguar to London to pick up the three co-conspirators. They then headed out on the M4 towards the Thames Valley, and after a 30-mile drive were soon in Maidenhead, Berkshire, where they pulled up outside the China Garden restaurant by Maidenhead Bridge, an upmarket establishment frequented by the local Chinese community and well-to-do English diners. They were taken into the restaurant where, seated at the back on a large circular table, were two thick-set Malaysians. After pleasantries were exchanged, they sat down to enjoy their complimentary feast and drinks.

Very quickly, the floodlight issue was raised and Liu was instructed to go with the others to Upton Park stadium within the next few days, and try to suss out the security at the ground. They were told to try to make contact with security personnel there, without raising suspicions, pretending that they were involved in the construction of a new stadium in the Far East, and to claim that they were checking out security arrangements in the UK so that their counterparts could take suggestions on board in the Far East. They were also told to pay particular attention to the floodlights at the ground, and try to establish where they were located and how they were operated. It was the floodlights, they were told, that were going to be targeted at this ground, and at other grounds too in the future. Liu was then handed a thick envelope, bulging with cash, for expenses. The envelope also contained false papers and laminated photo IDs, describing the trio as head of security for the Far Eastern Football Association. Within an hour, the three were speeding back to London, ready to put the plan into action.

Four days later, the three Chinese turned up at Upton Park football stadium. Properly known as the Boleyn Ground, home to West Ham United, the stadium had been built in 1904 and had a capacity for a crowd of 35,100. The gang of three had their first bit of good fortune when their bogus paperwork passed the cursory inspection of the ground's elderly security guard who was on duty all by himself and was keen to help his foreign guests. The trio were soon being shown round the grounds by the proud but naive guard, who believed he was acting in the best interests of promoting the stadium internationally. Nothing could have been further from the minds of the three Chinese conspirators as they were shown round the offices and directors' suites, the director's boxes, and finally the electronics section that controlled the floodlights. Eng Hwa Lim, the electronics engineer, took particular interest in this aspect of the ground, and their second bit of good fortune that day came when he realised how simple the electronics were that controlled the floodlights at the stadium. The Upton Park security officer had unwittingly put in motion a plan that was to rake in millions for the Far-Eastern betting cartel.

Back in West London later that same evening, Lim excitedly explained to the others how easy it would be for him to break the circuit that controlled the floodlights with a simple homemade electronic device, and went to work in constructing just such a remote-controlled system that could be operated from the grandstands risk-free and discreetly, without any spectators noticing. The three men had no hesitation in passing this valuable information on to their paymasters.

Back in Malaysia, the criminal cartel were feeling rather pleased with themselves. Not only had they managed to recruit exactly the type of operatives they had been looking for, but they already had possibilities of various football matches in mind at Upton Park and other stadiums that fitted their bill perfectly. Stadiums that they were now assured could be secretly infiltrated by their Chinese counterparts in London, and matches where they could kill the lights at a moment's notice. All they had to do now was wait for an opportune fixture to take place; they could be confident of massive betting in Malaysia, and then get themselves to work to fix the result in their favour.

They didn't have long to wait. In November 1997, a perfect opportunity presented itself: West Ham were playing Crystal Palace at home at Upton Park, a match that would whet the appetites of the gambling-hungry punters back in the Far East.

Nobody in the 28,000 crowd took a blind bit of notice of the three casually dressed Chinese spectators in winter coats and scarves who arrived just before kick-off and mingled with the fans in the stands. Crystal Palace scored in the first half, and, during half-time, Eng Hwa Lim received a text message from Malaysia on his mobile phone. Crystal Palace leading into the second half suited the bets the Malaysians had taken very well, but a draw was an even better result. Lim was instructed to wait 30 minutes, and if there were no further goals to kill the lights half an hour into the second half, or to use his apparatus immediately if West Ham equalised. Twenty minutes into the second half West Ham scored the prized goal. And, 35 seconds later, Eng Hwa Lim put his right hand into the pocket of his overcoat, pressed the button on his remote control and plunged the players and crowds of Upton Park into darkness. The match was abandoned; the daring floodlight coup had worked. In Malaysia, the cartel watched the fiasco on Sky television and rubbed their hands with glee at the ease in which they had pulled it off. They had amassed millions of dollars in losing bets, and did not hesitate to send a couple of hundred thousand over to England the following morning to keep their men on their payroll and in funds, ready for the next coup.

Following their well-rehearsed ritual that had worked at Upton Park, and dressing again as overseas officials, the trio then attended Selhurst Park stadium, home to Crystal Palace. Upon being escorted around the grounds, Lim was delighted to see that the floodlights there were as vulnerable as those at Upton Park. Thanking the head of security for showing them round the stadium, they then waited for their next instruction.

This time, the targeted match was Wimbledon vs. Arsenal at Selhurst Park almost a month after the West Ham match, and again, for Malaysian betting purposes, a draw after half-time was the ideal result. Lim duly put the lights out shortly after half-time, when the scores were level. Many more millions zoomed into the Malaysian betting cartel's coffers. The conspirators decided to call it a day for the time being, not wishing to push their luck too far, and a further £300,000 was sent over to the UK to line the pockets of Liu and co – making their pay packet so far £500,000 – and to keep them fresh and keen for a possible future coup.

In November 1998, the Malaysian cartel were at it again. This time they decided to target Charlton Athletic Football Club's stadium, known as The Valley. On instructions from their paymasters, the trio yet again attended the ground as foreign football security officials, complete with updated fake ID and official-looking letters of introduction, and were greeted by Charlton's head of security, Roger Firth. Firth showed them around the grounds, but the floodlight equipment at Charlton was inaccessible and housed in a secure area, which meant that the trio would need some help from the inside. The gang decided to bribe Firth, and put him in for a share of the action. Firth was a greedy man and had no hesitation in accepting a bung of £20,000. Liverpool were due to play Charlton on 13 February 1998, and Firth made arrangements to let the three gang members into the grounds on the evening of 10 February, so they could plant electronic equipment close to the floodlights, in order to make their plan, and Lim's remote control, work.

A few days beforehand, however, Firth became concerned that the second security guard at Charlton, who was also due to be on duty on 10 February and on the night of the match, could potentially cause difficulties for the team, so he took the decision to let him in on the coup, and part with £5,000 to buy his silence – and also to ensure that he stayed on the switchboard while the club's floodlights were tampered with. This was a clumsy attempt to bribe a security guard and unfortunately for the gang he went straight to the police, handed in his £5,000 booty and told them everything he knew about the plot. After sifting through his statement, the police decided that they ought to attend the match, and provide the gang with a surprise reception party.

On the evening of 10 February 1999, four men were arrested at the deserted Charlton Athletic Football Club grounds. Wai Yuen Liu, Chee Kew Ong, Eng Hwa Lim and Roger Firth were all taken into custody by the police three days before the match they were going to fix had even kicked off. A thorough search by the police revealed remote-control devices and other equipment – sufficient material, in fact, to wreck the lights at another eight games. They also found a magazine cutting from an electrical store and discovered the names of another two key individuals in the Charlton conspirators' personal belongings; one was employed at Upton Park, and the other at Selhurst Park. These two men were also arrested, but avoided charges because of a lack of concrete evidence.

The case went to trial at Middlesex Guildhall Crown Court in front of Judge Fabyan Evans and a jury. The security guard Firth pleaded guilty at an earlier hearing and turned Queen's evidence against his three Far-Eastern co-conspirators in exchange for a lighter sentence. He was to be the Crown's chief prosecution witness. The police went to great lengths to secure a conviction, even going to the trouble of erecting a miniature football stadium in the courtroom, complete with floodlights. Police electronics expert Mark Stokes then used a simple remote-control unit to turn the floodlights off, convincing the jury that the use of a remote control hidden in an overcoat pocket was indeed a reliable means of turning off football-stadium floodlights, a possibility the prosecuting barrister invited the jury to believe and accept.

The case against the trio was beginning to strengthen. During the trial, it emerged that Liu was a convicted fraudster with links to the Triad underworld. The jury didn't take long to return their guilty verdicts. Sentencing the four men, the judge told them, 'It is quite clear from the sums of money that have been in evidence that not only were other persons intending to scoop financial winnings, but all of you stood to gain substantial financial rewards.'

Ong and Lim were sentenced to four years' imprisonment each, Liu received 30 months and Firth got 18 months.

We can safely say that crime certainly didn't pay for these four individuals, who had been sentenced to 12 years' imprisonment for their involvement in the floodlight football scam. However, it's worth remembering that, in the Far East, the corrupt Malaysian betting cartel got away with their illegal millions scot-free.

The £1 Million Ritz
Casino Scam

Budapest, 16 September 2002, 12.31am

Very shortly after finishing a banquet fit for kings, held in the romantic setting of a medieval castle at Ráckeve on the river Danube just outside Budapest, the mathematics professor from the University of Technology and Economics (Hungary's equivalent of Massachusetts Institute of Technology) found himself rather overly refreshed. Three empty Cristal champagne bottles adorned the long mahogany table in the beautifully appointed dining room where he had enjoyed an eight-course feast with a couple of dozen other invited dignitaries, VIPs and aspiring businessmen from the new Eastern Bloc. Massive antique oil paintings in ornate gilt frames graced the walls; deep-red, heavy drapes with gold tassels flirted with the castle windows; huge ebony wax candles flickered in ostentatious holders; the crockery was the finest France could offer; and they had sipped vintage wines and champagnes all evening from Baccarat-crystal stemmed glasses.

Serving staff in crisp black-and-white uniforms were clearing away the remains from the table while a few young businessmen in dinner jackets, their black bow ties loosened, were lounging in their dining chairs, relaxed and laughing among themselves like school children, puffing away on thick Cohiba cigars and enjoying the finest cognacs and Armagnacs from massive brandy balloons. This was the reformed, nouveau-riche Budapest, and it smelled of money and power. A far cry from the Communist regime that Hungary had endured for decades.

The professor was now experiencing slight difficulty in standing, but at the same time he couldn't take his eyes off a gorgeous Hungarian woman who for some reason had decided to stay behind while most of the other guests had departed in their top-of-the-range imported Italian and German sports cars. He was trying desperately to find an opportune moment to chat her up, make small talk or simply get near to her. She was exquisitely attired in a silk off-the-shoulder dark-blue Frank Usher evening dress, impossibly high heels and what looked like a rather expensive diamond-and-sapphire necklace with matching earrings.

Despite being in his early fifties, and sporting wire-rim spectacles and greying hair, the professor still fancied himself as a bit of a ladies' man and had a pretty impressive track record for a man of his age. He also had a powerful secret weapon in his armoury that he was ready to unleash on this unsuspecting beauty to impress her. He had perfected a wonderful creation capable of making untold fortunes for anyone willing to listen to him and invest a little money: a miniature hi-tech James Bond-style computer device capable of predicting the outcome of a spin of a roulette wheel at a moment's notice. This invention, which he had created himself, was so clever that it was capable of beating the casinos at their own 'impossible to beat' game: American roulette.

The professor had always enjoyed dabbling with the complicated mathematical and logistical equations relating to gambling and statistics. He had built himself up a decent pension fund by predicting correctly the direction of the stock markets in Europe over the previous five years and was now convinced that he was about to make even greater fortunes from his invention. He had stumbled upon his theory of how to beat the roulette wheel almost by accident. Having devised a method of calculating velocity, speed and direction, he had gone on to work out a way of eliminating 31 of the 37 numbers of a roulette wheel as losers. In effect, the professor had managed to cut the odds of roulette in the punter's favour, from 37 to 1 to 6 to 1 – an unbelievable achievement, virtually guaranteeing financial success. Frequent trial runs on a full-sized casino roulette wheel in his dining room at home had produced regular, extremely profitable results, and he was desperate to share his discovery with someone – not only for the sake of his ego, but for the sake of the money that could be made. Maybe this Hungarian beauty had the key to unlocking the door of fortune for him?

He was now close enough to smell her perfume. Probably Chanel No.5, but definitely something expensive. She was even more stunning close up, naturally beautiful and about five foot nine. High cheekbones, pale, lightly powdered complexion and startling, dark-blue eyes that matched the sapphires in her necklace perfectly. He started chatting with her, they joked, they flirted, and then he lowered his guard and virtually blurted out the whole story of his invention. Far from being bored with what he had to say, she seemed genuinely interested. She let him finish the whole story at his own pace without interruption, and then she asked a few sensible and pertinent questions. He was delighted he had homed in on such a smart cookie, and was chuffed he had taken the initiative. By the time he had finished, she was interested enough to have swapped phone numbers and she promised to be in touch. He was sure he hadn't pulled, but was savvy enough to know he had whetted her appetite as far as the roulette gadget was concerned. He just hoped she had contacts that might be able to assist in his plan, and that she would get back in touch as promised.

He didn't have long to wait. Ten days later, shortly after lunchtime, the phone rang in his hallway. It was her. She sounded excited, almost childlike. Over the intervening few days, she had talked over his invention in detail with a couple of wealthy Serbian friends of hers, and they were interested in meeting him to take things further. She made it quite clear that, if the professor could deliver what he claimed, there was some serious money waiting for him. These Serbians were no slouches when it came to business, and were very streetwise. Trying to conceal his excitement, he made an appointment to see them all at his home that afternoon. He could hardly wait.

Two hours later, the beautiful woman and her two Serbian accomplices pulled up at the professor's house on the outskirts of Budapest in a brand-new, metallic-black, top-of-the-range Mercedes saloon to see the device in action for themselves. Set up in the dining room was a full-size roulette table, complete with chips, along with a friend of the professor's – a dealer from the local casino who had taken the day off by phoning in sick. He had been instructed to spin the wheel exactly as he did at work every day. The professor held in his hand what appeared to be a mobile phone, although it was only a prototype and was far from cosmetically perfected – there was no back to it and the batteries and wires were exposed. He instructed the dealer to spin the roulette wheel. The room went quiet. The professor stood about three feet away from the wheel, holding the device. Literally seconds before the ball was about to drop, a set of six numbers flashed up on the screen of the 'phone'. The team looked on in awe, as one of the six numbers on the screen was that of the number on the wheel where the ball had landed. The professor's device had actually calculated the velocity and speed of the ball and had predicted, within four neighbouring numbers, exactly which section of the wheel the ball would land in. They repeated the exercise a couple of dozen times, and every time, save one, the device was spot on.

Unbelievably excited at the potential of what they were witnessing, the three practised placing chips on the appropriate numbers on the layout in time before the ball landed, and after a while they got the grasp of the table's numbering sequence and soon were able to get their bets on without looking as though they were in a hurry. As seasoned gamblers, the two Serbians knew they were on to a sure winner and were already calculating the potential money they could make with the device. They agreed to meet the professor again as soon as possible, and to give him time to modify the device slightly so that it could actually be hidden inside a real mobile phone. They made it quite plain to him that a large fee would be paid for the finished device. And they wanted it as soon as possible. Both parties were now extremely keen to get the device spot on and move forward. They were painfully aware that there must be other people trying to simulate the same piece of equipment, so time was of the essence.

The professor worked round the clock, trimming here, shaving there, modifying and streamlining. He was very conscious that the device had to be so well concealed that it looked like an ordinary mobile phone, and would not raise any suspicion. Some of the casinos, he understood, had airport-style detector devices installed at reception, so the gadget had to be designed well enough to pass close scrutiny. A couple of weeks later, he was ready for them and, just 15 days after their original meeting, the gang met up with the professor again, parted with an agreed 140,000 Euros in cash, and left the professor's house with their 'mobile phone' and their key to untold riches. The professor decided to lie low for a while, and promptly booked himself a first-class one-way ticket to Barbados.

Now the hard work began. The team had to practise using their phone in proper casinos to make sure the device was viable in that environment, and also to make sure they could get the bets on without arousing suspicion on all six numbers in a hurry before the ball dropped. They were not short of choices of locations, either. The new Hungary was buzzing with money, and casinos were opening one after the other to relieve the new-style businessmen of their ill-gotten gains.

It was on their third visit to an upmarket casino in Budapest that the gang got their break. By sheer fluke, they noticed that at one of the higher-stakes roulette tables you could announce to the croupier what is known as a neighbour's bet. This is a call bet, declared to the croupier before or during the spin, amounting to a bet on a chosen number and also on the two numbers either side of it on the roulette wheel. This was designed as an insurance bet for a gambler who wanted to back a particular number on the wheel, but wanted to cover the two numbers either side of it in case the croupier just missed. Now, mercifully, the gang didn't have to worry about placing bets themselves in the hurry-up on six numbers and all the fiddling that went with it before the ball landed; they simply called the middle number that popped up on the screen and let the croupier do the work for them, covering the called number and the two either side of it for them on the wheel. True, one number would be missing from the equation, but that was a small price to pay for the comfort and security of the call bet. And, to disguise the bet further, they made other call bets as well, for lower stakes, to keep the croupier and management guessing. They had hit the jackpot, and they were determined to milk it for all it was worth.

What's more, to their delight, they noticed, on certain tables, that there was even a 'racetrack' of all the roulette numbers in exactly the same sequence as the numbers were spaced out on the wheel, for the croupier's convenience, so that the dealer only had to place their wager on the number called on his racetrack, take note of where the ball dropped and then divide the wager into five and place the chips on the winning number after the spin, should it be a winner – which, of course, it was – producing a payout of a cool 35–1!

Over the next year or more, the gang of three worked the coup meticulously in the casinos of Budapest until their system, clever betting tricks and disguises and general wagering skills were perfected. They were careful not to go every night, and they took turns over who kept the phone, first hiding the phone in the breast pocket of one of the Serbians' shirts, then the other Serbian's jacket top pocket, and finally in the girl's handbag. They went to great lengths to ensure that their investment was protected. Back at home, day after day, they practised a complicated and almost unnoticeable system of signals among themselves to indicate which number was due to come up. They took their turns in making the bets, concealing the phone, and sometimes even placed moody bets on the layout to disguise what they were up to and confuse the casino staff, managers and security personnel. Although they were playing for moderately low stakes, the team were aware that their phenomenal run of success would cause immediate suspicion, so they were very careful to move from casino to casino, often signing in with false passports and IDs, and towards the end of the practice year even went to the lengths of wearing disguises. On one particular evening, they all nearly cracked up as the one female member of the gang turned up to 'work' dressed as a guy, complete with false moustache and ID!

By February 2004, after more than a year of practice, the gang of three were ready to swoop on a major London casino and go for the chandeliers. They had already amassed more than the equivalent of £100,000 in winnings from their practice sessions in Budapest, which had given them a comfortable lifestyle and also provided the means for upping the ante in London, while, of course, as the woman in particular noted with delight, living the high life in the English capital at the same time.

London Heathrow Airport, 11 March 2004, 11.35am
On this drizzly March morning, no other travellers took much notice of the three casually dressed Eastern Europeans who had flown economy, landed at Heathrow airport and cabbed it to an upmarket five-star hotel in the West End. They booked into three separate penthouse suites and, after unpacking, met in the bar on the first floor of the hotel to enjoy a lunchtime refresher, celebrate their arrival in London with vintage champagne and toast their impending success at the roulette tables of

some unsuspecting casino in London. The following day, they started an orgy of spending in the designer boutiques in the West End, the two boys blitzing Armani, Versace and Valentino, while the girl peeled off thousands at the Knightsbridge branches of Karen Millen and Joseph.

That evening, they dined at San Lorenzo, and again clinked champagne glasses to their anticipated success. Poring over a listing of all the major London casinos at dinner, they decided that the Ritz Casino was to be their target and fine-tuned the timing of the plot: they were going to go to work there in four days' time. So, after a few more days of shopping, eating in the finest restaurants and pampering themselves at the best hairdressers and beauty salons, they were ready for action. The coup was about to commence.

Ritz Casino, London, 15 March 2004, 11.48pm
It was at precisely this time that a group of three chic punters, two Serbian men aged 38 and 33 and a 32-year-old Hungarian woman, walked into the Ritz Casino in London. Cameras from reception, the hallway and casino entrance monitored and recorded their movements as they made their way down the thick carpet of the sumptuously appointed boulevard to the casino proper. Once inside, the

sophisticated 'eye in the sky' video surveillance would closely record every movement, word uttered, chip handled and bet placed.

The Ritz Casino is one of the world's most exclusive, respected and highly powered gambling houses, their exclusive rooms tucked away off London's Piccadilly in the former ballroom of the hotel. Here, at this popular haunt for Arab princes and international playboys, high rollers are pampered with complimentary gourmet food and wine, fine champagnes and the best Havana cigars. Even courtesy limousines are provided to ferry punters to and from the smartest hotels and apartments in the capital, where the day after play bouquets of flowers, magnums of champagne and tins of caviar are delivered with the casino manager's compliments. In these plush surroundings, hardly an eyebrow is raised when gamblers change up tens of thousands of pounds to wager on blackjack and roulette.

However, the Ritz Casino is no stranger to controversy. In 2002, they took one of their high-rolling clients, a Mr al-Zayat, to court for bouncing $3 million worth of cheques that he had issued for gambling chips. (In fairness, that happened after he had lost about $17 million over more than 150 visits to the casino between 1999 and 2001.) The High Court found in the Ritz's favour and froze Mr al-Zayat's assets, including a Boeing jet and a Rolls-Royce, as well as his bank accounts in Switzerland, the Isle of Man and Cyprus.

But when these three Eastern European scammers walked into the Ritz that evening, it was business as usual. They headed straight for a high-stakes roulette table that accepted call bets and changed up £10,000 in cash in £50 notes into high-value gambling chips. An inspector looked on, arms folded. They let the croupier spin a couple of times while they fiddled about with a few call bets for fun, and then they got down to the proper work.

That evening the woman had the 'phone' in her handbag and she stood some distance from the end of the roulette table by the wheel itself. Through an elaborate method of very discreet hand signals that they had perfected over the previous year and a half, which included the woman running her hand through her hair (signifying number 3), or folding her arms (number 11), she would signal the middle number that flashed up on the mobile in her bag to her. This gave the others just enough time to place their call bet on the winning numbers. The croupier spun the ball slowly anticlockwise while the wheel rotated in the opposite direction, and they got their signal for number 22. 'Twenty-two and the neighbours by five hundred,' they growled at the dealer as they flung over £2,500 in high-value chips. Bingo! Thirty-one, black. Neighbours win. The Ritz croupier placed the £500 chip straight up on the winning number, and slid their winnings of £17,500 across the green baize. Next was 11, same result. Followed by 30, 29, 2 and 14. Time to stop. System working well, no need to be greedy. Everything going to plan. They had just won over £100,000 in less than ten minutes. Their system worked, the signalling was spot on and no one had noticed; hardly anyone raised an eyebrow, either, when they went to the cash cage to draw their winnings. They had just completed the first night of a well-rehearsed scam that was intended to take the casino for many, many millions.

Ritz Casino, London, 16 March 2004, 10.18pm
The following evening, the gang of three returned. After attending swiftly to a bottle of complimentary vintage champagne, they were soon back at the roulette table. Casino management, now taking slightly more of an interest in them, were delighted when the gang started changing up the sealed packets of £50 notes that they had won the previous evening into high-value chips, although at this stage they were just considered to be lucky tourists who

had got it right and were about to give it all back, and more. Or so the management thought.

Coincidentally, one of the croupiers dealing the roulette at the Ritz that evening was also from Budapest, although he was only unwittingly part of the coup and was not known to the gang, or them to him. Had he uttered the words 'Holgyeim es uraim, tegyek meg fogadasukat, senki tobbet' instead of 'Place your bets', he might have succeeded in putting the gang off their stride – for by this time they had become well known to Hungarian gambling experts, and had been banned from all the top Budapest casinos *in absentia*.

But the gang of three were exuding enormous confidence after their trial run the previous evening, and pressed up their winnings. Over the next 45 minutes, they (naturally) kept hitting their numbers, spin after spin. Even their 'throwinsky' guess bets had produced a profit for them! The casino, now aware that they were haemorrhaging chips at an alarming rate, tried every tactic available to them to stem the tide of high-value plaques moving over the baize. They changed croupier after virtually every spin. They changed the ball. Their men in suits came and stood by the table, arms folded, to put the gang off. But their chip stack simply kept multiplying, and, on their final spin, they were signalled 31, number 9 obliged (next door) and they had amassed in excess of £1 million of winnings – their agreed predetermined cut-off point.

Back at the cashier's cage, they were handed £300,000 in cash and a cheque for £900,000. But the casino authorities were now very suspicious about this incredible run of luck, and, as soon as the trio left, management and security discussed their suspicions that the gang were working for an East European syndicate, and somehow had managed to find a way to beat the wheel. But how? Intense viewing of the surveillance tapes gave nothing away, so the Ritz concluded that the gang must be using a sophisticated state-of-the-art scanner, probably hidden in a mobile phone, to predict the outcome of selected spins. They further surmised that, in between these selected spins, in order to avoid closer scrutiny and suspicion, the gang were simply making regular bets, guessing, and hoped to get lucky. There could be no other legitimate explanation.

The closer the casino management and security department (made up mainly of ex-Scotland Yard officers) studied the tapes, the more convinced they became that they had been had over. These scanners had been known to the casino for some time, and they understood they measured the speed of the roulette ball as the croupier released it, identified where it fell and measured the declining orbit of the wheel. The data was then beamed to the microcomputer hidden in the phone and flashed on to the phone, giving the trio just enough time to place their bets on all the six numbers in the section where the ball would end up.

By first light that morning, the casino had decided that it was going to thwart the gang's attempts at any more easy pickings. First, it would place a 'stop' instruction at the bank for the cheque it had issued for £900,000. Second, it would call in Scotland Yard. Unluckily, however, the cashier at the Ritz had erroneously assumed that their bank opened at 9.30am – when in fact they opened at nine on the dot – so, by the time she telephoned the stop instruction through, it was too late.

The police had rushed round to the Ritz's bank in the West End but were too late for the gang, who had presented the cheque for payment the minute the bank had opened at nine, and had had it cleared into their own account before the branch were even aware of the casino's stop instruction. Heads were about to roll. But the money wouldn't be staying in the gang's account for too long.

By a sheer fluke, one of the Serbians had left some paperwork, on which he had done some calculations, screwed up on the counter with their hotel's name and address on it, so the police, putting two and two together, were able to rush round to the hotel and nab them. They already had printed-out mugshots of who they were looking for, courtesy of the Ritz, and they also asked the bank to keep their CCTV tapes as evidence. At the hotel, the three were arrested, their hotel rooms searched, and their 'mobile phone' seized. The bulk of their £400,000 winnings was also confiscated. After a quick and successful application by CPS barristers in the High Court in the Strand that same morning, the gang's bank account was frozen with the £900,000 in it. The three were also required to hand over their passports.

After hours of interviews at the local police station, the trio were released on bail pending an investigation into 'allegations of obtaining money by deception through gambling'. The arrests made headline news in that evening's papers. The security department at the Ritz were desperate for a conviction, and a long sentence. They were still reeling after the episode with Mr al-Zayat, which had caused them huge embarrassment in the gaming community. They were desperate to reassert themselves as the market leaders and to demonstrate to the world that the Ritz was not easy pickings.

The Ritz Casino scam, however, did not elicit much surprise in Budapest gambling circles. Sandor

Bikali, Varkert Casino's manager, commented, 'We too have had gamblers who have been caught red-handed using similar gadgets abroad. The woman involved in the London incident is on our casino's blacklist here and is not welcome in our club.'

The Hungarian casino's security department had been trained to up the ante against cheats, card counters and chip scammers. He also confirmed that the alleged laser scanner device was being used in Hungary, and outlined how it worked. 'The operating principle of the gadget is relatively simple,' he explained. 'A laser beam measures one position of the inert ball, say on 31, then when the ball is spun it measures its speed, tracks its movement and works out its likely landing spot. The accuracy of the device is awesome.'

The casinos, not only in Hungary but also the rest of the world, knew that they had to keep up with the advent of technology in order to protect their sacred cow of profit margin. They had quickly got to work, swapping and sharing information, and emailing profiles of any suspicious punters to each other, so they could be barred from entering at the door.

Meanwhile, back in London, the police and the Crown Prosecution Service now went into top gear to formulate charges and prosecute the trio. The police felt they had a watertight case. The gang had been caught almost red-handed, the cash had been seized and there were tapes of video evidence. But the police hadn't fully appreciated that anyone accused of cheating in a British casino has a real sporting chance of getting away with it, because they can only be prosecuted under the Gaming Act of 1845 – and this archaic law is blind to state-of-the-art gadgets. In a further complication, the trio had not violated any modern-day law, as the scanner had not interfered with the ball or the wheel. So, although they had walked away with over a cool £1 million, it seemed that the chances of a successful prosecution were actually rather remote after all.

Finally, nine months later, and after long consultation with the top lawyers of the Crown Prosecution Service, the police reluctantly conceded there was no case to answer, and they had no choice but to formally release the trio without charge, return their property and cash to them, and allow them to freely roam in and out of the country. (To make matters worse, it later emerged that three other London casinos had fallen victim to the same scam, but had decided not to publicise the fact.)

The Budapest Three had audaciously pulled off one of the biggest betting scams ever, getting away scot-free with over £1,125,000.

8

The £10 Million Halifax
IOU Thief

Everyone assumes that financial consultants, bankers, brokers and investment advisors have their clients' interests at heart, that they are scrupulously honest when it comes to handling said clients' funds and that they wouldn't dare dip into the client's account. While this is normally so – and, in most cases, the general public are protected to some extent by the Financial Services Act and the compensation scheme that is attached to it – it always comes as a bit of a shock, to put it mildly, when it turns out that the person offering financial advice is a common thief and conman. When the amount of money swindled reaches the incredible figure of £10 million, shock turns to anger, dismay and disbelief. Understandably, the public then become angry, blame everyone but themselves and cannot believe their own naivety.

Precisely such a scenario occurred when Graham Price, a manager of the Halifax Building Society franchise branch in the village of Gowerton, situated some five miles westwards from the city of Swansea, went on tilt. Price was trusted with substantial sums of customers' savings, and conducted everyday banking and financial transactions on behalf of the Halifax from his office. The motto of the Halifax is 'always giving you Xtra' and Graham Price's customers were certainly going to be delivered 'extra'. Much more 'extra', in fact, than they had ever bargained for.

It is often said that conmen have more front than Harrods, and in this case the Halifax front lent an ideal air of respectability to Graham Price's other business, which was that of an investment advisor, a business that he conducted from his private suite in the same building as the Halifax office. The rotund, grey-haired Price had a reputation as a quiet man locally, a solid man, a man you could trust. He wasn't loud or showy, and went about his business almost unnoticed. The perfect front for what he had going on in his crooked mind.

From Price's point of view, the beauty of operating from a Halifax office as an independent private financial advisor was that he had access to all Halifax's clients' personal details, including complete profiles of their financial worth, stored and easily accessible on the Halifax computer. He could see at an instant who had what in their accounts, and which clients had policies and endowments that were about to mature. He could even tell which of his clients had just enjoyed a touch in the stock market. Armed with all this information, Price got to work on targeting the wealthiest of the Halifax's customers, inviting them to attend his private office for a confidential chat about their finances. Once he had a client in the net, Price offered to switch their savings at the Halifax into a land-leasehold scheme that sounded very convincing, looked great on paper and, like all Ponzi schemes, offered his clients a magnificent rate of return, on paper at least. (The term 'Ponzi scheme' is named after a scam by Charles Ponzi in the 1920s, in which he enlisted people to invest in a project for a guaranteed return, using money given by later subscribers to pay off those who had invested earlier on.) Price didn't just *tempt* his clients – he had them all hopelessly hooked. He offered them up to 25 per cent interest per annum on their investments, and promised to credit the money quarterly to their accounts at the Halifax. An incredible rate of return, by any standards.

As he grew in confidence, his chutzpah knew no bounds. It later transpired that one day Benjamin Evans, a 76-year-old pensioner and a long-standing customer of the Halifax, had walked into the branch to conduct a small transaction. Price swooped, invited him into his office for a cup of tea and convinced him to invest his money in his bogus land deal. Unfortunately, Evans agreed and handed over his life savings of £160,000 there and then on the spot. The following day, Price cornered Maureen Finn, an elderly widow, who naively handed over her money too. She was to lose over £125,000 as a result. Price also conned her into handing over a further £8,000 after he claimed £40,000 had been stolen from his car. Probably the most audacious target he chose was one of his own cashiers, 52-year-old Jennifer Ellis, who lost a six-figure sum. Her aunt Mabel Fletcher, 86, was also a big loser, after paying in £217,000. In order to benefit from this complicated financial arrangement Price had constructed, most of the victims were asked to keep their business arrangements with him confidential – for reasons that soon become painfully apparent.

Price convinced his clients to invest their

redundancy money, pension payments and life savings into his scheme, and even persuaded some to remortgage their homes in order to raise more cash. Suzie Mills invested £500,000 with Graham Price after he promised her big returns. She sold her flourishing Bed and Breakfast and her home to bankroll the venture. Now, her dream of setting up a private healing centre in retirement has turned into a daily grind of fighting to make ends meet. Ms Mills, 58, of Honiton, Devon, now lives in a rented flat, struggles to pay her bills and has a low-income job in a nursing home. 'I've been very near to cracking up,' she admitted recently. 'My life has been totally destroyed.' She had even advised a friend to invest his life savings in Price's scheme. The friend died soon after of cancer, but was troubled to the end by how he would cope. 'The last few months of his life were extremely unpleasant,' Ms Mills revealed. 'It's all been a nightmare, an absolute nightmare.'

Price even went as far as to persuade some of his own friends to invest, people he had known and who had trusted him for at least twenty years.

Within a few months, Price had £3,368,479 under his management from 84 unsuspecting victims for his land-leaseback deal. To start with, he paid the depositors the interest on their investments, every quarter, as promised – no doubt from the fresh funds that flowed in from the new investors, the classic Ponzi scheme modus operandi. However, Price had a very sinister hidden agenda. There was no land and there was no leasehold scheme. He was using his investors' money to finance a habit he had that had grown completely out of control. Graham Price was using those funds he had under management to satisfy his addiction to horse racing, betting and racehorse ownership. He used the cash to buy a £250,000 stake in 13 racehorses, and paid racing tipsters he saw advertise in the *Racing Post* an astonishing £1.7 million for tips during the course of his scam. Many of these tipsters were conmen themselves, and had little difficulty in extracting huge sums from Price for worthless information and the promise of big-priced winners at the racetrack.

One tipster from Brighton performed the ultimate con on him. His name was Steve Phrobisher, and he tipped Price a horse on a Monday, which was fully expected to win, and told Price to have his boots on it as an introduction to his exclusive racing information service. The horse duly won by three lengths, pulling the proverbial cart, and Price enjoyed a healthy pay day. The very next day, Steve the tipster phoned Price again. 'We've just had one in Ireland, I didn't have time to phone you, so I put five grand on it for you. It's bolted up at 2–1, and I'm sending you a registered package with ten grand in readies in it. Keep the money safe. I've got another one at the weekend we can have a proper touch on, the best of the bunch, and it will probably SP at 4–1 or bigger.'

Steve the tipster sent Price his ten grand. Of course, there was no winner in Ireland at all – this was money he was using to invest in Price's emotion and to speculate on his greed. Steve knew that Price was now hopelessly in awe of him, and the ten grand would be kept to one side by Price, ready for the next touch. Steve knew he would soon be getting it back, plus a large bundle more.

On the Thursday, Steve was on the phone to Price again, in hushed tones. 'Can you speak? I've got the green light. This horse is off on Saturday in Ireland. It's a bent race, and the horse will definitely win. I have been asked to get a hundred grand on for the connections, the owner, the trainer and the jockey. How much of it can you handle? Call me back as soon as you can. I've got other clients who I can do this with, but I want to give you a chance. But remember, I need to have the cash by Friday afternoon at the latest, as it has to be in Ireland by Saturday morning to be distributed round the bookies. We're going to make 400 per cent. Here's my private number. Call me back as soon as you can.'

Of course, the phone number that Steve gave him was a pay-as-you-go mobile number that could be disposed of at a moment's notice.

Back in Gowerton, Graham Price sat down in his office and had a think. He would dearly like to have the whole coup to himself. Steve had already trusted him with the ten grand, and had tipped him two winners on the bounce that had (apparently) won their races easily. True, he hadn't actually seen the Irish race, he only had Steve's excited account of it to go on. But he did have the ten grand, so it must have won... He now set about thinking how he could get his hands on the extra ninety grand in a day. Simple: he would order it from the Halifax, make out it was for a customer, and have it delivered to the branch the following morning. He made a mental note to keep tabs of all the money he was helping himself to from the Halifax, but nobody seemed to be taking a blind bit of notice.

He phoned Steve, who was propping up the bar at one of Hove's exclusive watering holes, quaffing champagne. 'I'll have the 100k for you tomorrow lunchtime.'

'Great,' said Steve. 'I'll have someone come and collect it from your offices. Large notes if you can, Graham, got to get them over to Ireland in a private plane in one go.'

The following lunchtime, one of Steve's co-conspirators arrived at Graham Price's offices in Gowerton. He had been primed for his task, was extremely well spoken and turned out, and ready for any eventuality. After introducing himself, he was led into Price's office, where there were four large brown envelopes on the desk, each containing £25,000 in crisp new £50 notes with Halifax paper bands around them.

'Got you large notes, like your boss asked for,' Price said as he handed over the four envelopes.

'Great, it makes life easier for the boys who have to go over to Ireland. This money has to be spread all over the country tomorrow. I'll be back to see you on Monday, with the winnings. Then we'll have time for a chat, and maybe a little celebratory drink? Be seeing you.'

And exactly five minutes and fifteen seconds after walking into Price's office, the young conman was walking out with a hundred large, in fifties, with Halifax paper bands around them, ready to be divvied up in Hove that evening over expensive champagne to celebrate the conmen's best coup yet.

The following afternoon, a frustrated Price tried ringing Steve to see how his horse had got on, and wondered why his private number was unobtainable. Then the penny dropped. Realising he had been had,

Price went out and bought a top-of-the-range Mercedes to console himself, his first venture into luxury goods during his murky double-dealings. Friends and clients in Gowerton who noticed a change in Price's behaviour – his flash cars and expensive holidays – could have been forgiven for thinking that he had just won the lottery. Most thought he was going through a mid-life crisis. He even bought hundreds of thousands of pounds' worth of shares and premium bonds for his children. But nothing could have been further from the truth: he was, in fact, digging himself deeper and deeper in debt and, when the £3 million he had milked from his investors ran out, he simply started helping himself from the Halifax itself.

Price had an incredible appetite for online gambling, wagering some £7 million with the online firm of Fred Done, and, as a keen buyer of bloodstock, had syndicated shares in 11 horses including River Bug, Hammer of the Gods, One in the Eye, Bumblefly, Dodger and Mujalia. He was also a regular at Cheltenham and Chester racecourses, where he would bet in thousands – with the Halifax's cash. Soon he had borrowed nearly £7 million from the Halifax. IOUs are normally not worth the paper they are written on, but in order to cover his tracks, and take any blame away from his staff, he left an

IOU in the firm's safe. Neatly written, appropriately enough on the back of a Halifax compliments slip, the IOU stated, 'I Graham Price have borrowed £7 million from the Halifax float.'

Over a period of just four years, Graham Price had managed to get through the guts of £10 million. He had used the money to gamble at the racetrack and on the internet, to buy share portfolios and premium bonds for his family, a couple of Mercedes cars, holidays in the US and Portugal, shares in racehorses, a fitted kitchen and to pay off mortgages. His elaborate four-year scam was only uncovered when an auditor for the Halifax, Leslie Tucker, arrived at the Gowerton branch unannounced to carry out a spot check. Price was enjoying an expensive holiday in New York at the time, again paid for with stolen cash, and Tucker was told by the innocent and naive staff that there was a float of £7 million in the safe – which Tucker thought quite bizarre, to say the least. Upon opening the safe, Tucker discovered three shoeboxes. Two contained empty envelopes, the other the soon-to-become-infamous IOU.

Graham Price swiftly became known as the 'IOU thief' and of great interest to the police. Upon arriving back in the country from the United States, he was arrested – as was his wife, son and three Halifax employees.

At the police station, Price admitted everything, telling the detectives, 'Just give me a couple more weeks, I'll win it all back.'

At least the new tipsters he was dealing with had done a sterling job in convincing Price they had a coup lined up for him. Price was charged with theft, and bailed to appear at Swansea Crown Court. The others were found to be completely innocent and were released without charge.

In November 2005, Graham Price sat impassively in the dock, with his head bowed and his hands folded on his lap. He admitted 43 charges of theft and deception and asked for another 263 offences to be considered. There were gasps from the public gallery as around fifty of his victims, many in their seventies, eighties and even nineties, heard that the 58-year-old father of two had embarked on a spending spree after turning from respectable businessman to big-time swindler. He milked £3,368,479 from the investors and stole £6,950,000 from the Halifax. Prosecutor Chris Clee told the court that many of the victims were elderly investors who could ill afford the losses Price had loaded on them. Several, including Mr Evans, could now lose their homes, while others would have to start working again.

The police were not satisfied that all of the stolen

money had been accounted for and were still trying to trace more than £1.7 million that was missing. The web of deception was so complicated that the judge was forced to adjourn sentencing until the following day after hearing more than four hours of evidence about Price's offences, stretching from January 2001 until November 2004, when he was arrested by the police. The prosecutor went on to tell the court that Price admitted theft of all the money, which he said was used to feed his gambling habit. He had diverted £4 million into his own account at the Halifax in the space of just eleven weeks the previous year.

But then the police investigator in charge of the case, Richard Jones, dropped a bombshell on the court. Price hadn't *lost* £7 million gambling on the horses at all – he had *wagered* £7 million. The bets had returned over £6 million, leaving a net deficit of only £700,000. The policeman went on, 'On the face of things, it looked as if he was betting an extreme amount, but he did win sometimes, and was then putting the money back in... It was shown that he had £6 million winnings with BetFred in Warrington.'

'So the question remains on your mind, where has it gone?' said the judge.

'That's correct,' Mr Jones replied.

Later, it emerged that the Halifax had frozen victims' accounts and cleared them of cash, arguing that it was also a victim of Price's scam. A spokesman commented, 'There is no doubt these transfers were bogus. No money was deposited, these were simply entries to the accounts with no money to support them.'

When an internal bank inquiry established the vast majority of payments were bogus, balances were returned to zero to reflect that reality. But some investors said this made them feel victimised for a second time, by losing cash in their Halifax accounts as well as their investments.

A victims' group was set up with a view to making a legal challenge against the Halifax Bank in an attempt to recover some of the money they say they have lost. But the bank has stressed that it was also a victim and acted only to clear up discrepancies left by Price's fraud. It claims that cash apparently paid into the Halifax accounts of Price's victims was in fact never credited to them at all. In two cases, victims had removed money that did not exist and they had since been contacted and asked to pay it back. A statement released by the Halifax at the time read, 'As well as defrauding a number of his own clients, Mr Price stole a considerable amount of money from Halifax. Both Halifax and Mr Price's private clients are victims of his fraud. All investments made with Mr Price were paid either directly into his personal bank account or by cheque payable to him. Mr Price's clients deposited no money with Halifax in connection with these "investment accounts".' Further grief for the innocent victims.

However, several weeks after this announcement, and after pressure from the victims' solicitors and MPs, the financial giant the Halifax suddenly changed its stance and decided that it would make *ex-gratia* payments to those investors who have lost capital as a result of the fraud perpetrated by Graham Price, ensuring that they are put back in the position they were prior to their investing with Price. In addition, Halifax will pay investors a 'best buy' rate of interest (5 per cent) on their original investment.

Meanwhile, back at Swansea Crown Court, Graham Price was being sentenced. His barrister stated, 'He blames absolutely nobody, save himself.' The barrister actually mentioned as defence material in summing up that Price actually believed he could win the money back.

Sentencing him, Judge John Diehl observed, 'Any words of mine are almost bound to be inadequate to reflect the extent of your deceit... In my view, these were breaches of trust of the grossest order.' He noted that individual investors lost homes, pension nest eggs and inheritances to the bogus land scheme that had devastated their lives and left many in difficulty. As a result, many had been left with higher mortgages, or had been forced to sell their homes, while still others were forced to return to work rather than retire.

Graham Price received a prison sentence of 12 years – an unbelievably long sentence for a first offence of financial crime on an early guilty plea, though, if he receives a reduction at the Court of Appeal, it will receive far less publicity than the original sentence. And one fact still remains tantalisingly unaccounted for: Graham Price has taken the secret of those missing millions with him to his cell.

The Stock-Exchange
Insider-Dealing Scams

In the good old days of pre-regulation in the City of London, when jobbers, dealers and brokers all wore the old-school tie, almost anything and everything was possible as far as insider dealing and gambling on the markets with marked cards was concerned. And very few eyebrows were raised as long as the insiders didn't take too many liberties, shrouded their dealings in secrecy and kept the whole operation within the 'old boy' network. A bit of 'insider' gambling on the next takeover or set of results was just icing on the cake, the City's old-fashioned settlement terms and antiquated dealing practices giving the scammers plenty of scope for manoeuvre. Compared to the current regulated City of London – with its Chinese Walls, compliance officers and taped phone conversations – the City in the Seventies and Eighties was more like a financial Wild West.

The City, and the Stock Exchange in particular – often called the greatest casino in the world – was primed for scams, and many took place with alarming regularity. Looking back on it now, it's amazing that any outsiders actually made any money in the markets, with all the fiddling and diddling that went on. Many traders found themselves privy to insider information, and were quite happy to swap what they knew for the proverbial brown envelope. Many examples of insider trading took place – some unsophisticated, others concocted by geniuses – and one has to understand the serious extent of what was common practice in order to realise how easily some of these scams were perpetrated. Although many of them occurred regularly as recently as only twenty years ago, it is only really in the last decade or so that regulators have clamped down on insider dealing to any effective extent, as we shall see.

One common insider-dealing scam used to take place every Friday afternoon in City pubs and wine bars. Fleet Street journalists loved to frequent such establishments, often arriving for the start of their weekend at Friday lunchtime in an attempt to drink themselves into oblivion before their commute home to the suburbs. By about two o'clock, the bars were filling up with City traders, many from the Stock Exchange, who were also keen to down a few jars. But these traders also had an ulterior motive for knocking off early. They were keen to pal up with their Fleet Street counterparts in order to extract and pay for valuable information. They wanted to know, before the markets closed on the Friday afternoon, which stocks and shares were going to be tipped on the financial pages in the weekend newspapers. This information was incredibly easy to obtain by almost anyone who worked on Fleet Street, and could be touted by those in the know to those who wanted to be in the know – for a fee. Any share that was tipped in the City columns of a weekend newspaper was almost certain to rise in value on the Monday morning as soon as the Stock Market reopened after the weekend break. Brokers and traders who knew in advance which shares were being given the green light would simply buy as many as they could afford to on the Friday afternoon, wait for the weekend editions to appear and then sell their holding on the following Monday morning at a tidy profit. In these early days of insider dealing, one could purchase stocks and shares on credit, as a two-week accounting period existed. If you bought and sold equities during the two-week period and showed a profit, the brokers simply sent you your cheque on settlement day. It was very easy to obtain credit from brokers, and several of the old firms of stockbrokers went under by extending huge lines of credit to punters who didn't have the means to cover their losses when the market turned bearish against them.

Of course, the general public were being scammed with all this insider business going on – it was gambling with marked cards. Nobody seemed to care, though, and this weekend share-tipping ruse went on unchecked, week after week for years on end, earning fortunes for the dealers and brokers involved and lining the pockets of some Fleet Street hacks.

New issues (i.e. shares that are being issued for sale to the public for the first time) were another area where those in the know had an unfair advantage. Many of the new issues had a closing time of noon, and the smart players often used to make multiple applications for these, turning up at the issuing house at the last minute to see which institutions were subscribing for the shares. If the right players were getting involved, the 'stag' – as a new issues player was called – would hand in his applications, safe in the knowledge that the price would open up at a premium. You could sell the new issues at a profit, and get paid for them, before the issuing house had even presented your cheque for payment. Happy days!

Another popular scam involved information obtained from directors and employees of the companies quoted on the Stock Exchange itself. The most sensitive time for these companies was when results were about to be published, as this would indicate if they were about to be taken over by another firm, or were about to take over another company themselves. Results were very important in the City and highly regarded when it came to valuing a company's stock, with many well-paid analysts competing with each other to try and pre-guess how well or badly a company had fared over the previous trading year. Obviously, any help offered in this direction by dishonest finance directors was very valuable, and was well rewarded. Many jobbers, dealers and brokers in the City became intimate with the larger institutions and fund managers, and were very eager to learn at the earliest possible opportunity of any large investments the funds were about to make, and in which company.

There were rules of a sort in place to prevent all

this happening, but it was not until the 1980s that insider dealing was taken seriously, and rubber stamped on the statute books. In law, for someone to be guilty of insider dealing, they had to have used knowledge that was not in the public domain, was likely to affect the share price – in other words, was price sensitive – and the trader had to have used the information wittingly. If he passed the information on to a friend, even for free, he was still guilty of an offence. However, prosecutions were rare, and convictions even rarer, as the offences were so hard to prove.

Furthermore, there was a grey area about the distinction between directors' dealings, which were quite legal, and insider dealing. A shining example of how borderline the whole scenario was is well illustrated by the case of the directors of Tarmac Ltd, who built up their holding in their own company in late 1999. Tarmac's share price had been depressed for months over interest-rate fears, and the directors used this negativity to acquire huge holdings of shares in their own company at a bargain-basement price. Ironically, just one day after the final purchases were made by the directors, the price of Tarmac shares rallied by over 30 per cent on a takeover bid. The Stock Exchange was suspicious of the timing of the directors' purchases and instigated an immediate investigation, but the directors maintained they knew nothing of the bid, and had merely bought their own shares because they believed they were undervalued. After a Stock Exchange investigation, the directors were exonerated, but the message was clear: directors were putting their liberty in jeopardy if they dabbled with insider knowledge.

With the recent advent of spread betting and contracts for difference, the offence of insider trading became much more complex, as off-market trading transactions became subject to the law of insider trading as well.

Spread betting is a fairly recent form of gambling in the City. The attraction is that all profits are tax free – which isn't surprising, because most people lose. The Chancellor has certainly got that one right, taxing the firms that make the millions on spread betting, rather than chasing the few who get lucky. The attraction of spread betting for the gambling public is obvious – fairly tight spreads on indexes and stocks, as well as the ability to gamble on commodity, metal and energy markets. Directors and shareholders need to know the rules and how to avoid exposure to personal, criminal and civil liability. Very recently, an employee of Pace Micro Technology, one of the darling stocks of the 1990s, was fined £250,000 by the Financial Services Authority (FSA) for selling stock in his company when he knew in advance that a bid was about to be withdrawn.

Insider dealing, therefore, occurs when individuals or companies use, or allow others to use, price-sensitive information about a share that has been obtained through inside knowledge or contacts. The Stock Exchange itself has its own rules, which reinforce the law on insider trading, although they rarely enforce them, and when they do the matter is usually handed over to the FSA. Despite the fact that penalties for insider trading attract prison sentences of up to seven years, prosecutions are rare.

One famous case, however, deserves a mention. Probably encouraged by the fact that prosecutions and convictions for insider dealing are very rare, and ignoring the draconian penalties, Norman Payne, Richard Spearman, Michael Smith and Catherine Spearman decided to embark on an infamous orgy of insider dealing.

Norman Payne's job was that of a proofreader and he worked for a printing company called Burrups Ltd. One of Burrups' activities was to print secret and price-sensitive brochures for City mergers and takeovers. Many of these brochures were being printed at Burrups before the Stock Exchange had announced the takeover or merger, and therefore

Payne had access to hugely valuable information. He had no qualms about passing on the information in the brochures to his friends Michael Smith and Catherine Spearman, and they in turn informed Catherine's estranged husband Richard Spearman of the details. Richard Spearman then embarked on a buying frenzy of the shares in question, safe in the knowledge that he was on to a sure thing. Norman Payne was paid for supplying the information he'd gleaned, while Catherine Spearman and Smith took a cut of the action. This was insider dealing in its purest form.

The gang profited from 27 takeover and merger transactions. However, celebrations of their good fortune was short-lived as they were quickly discovered and charged with conspiracy and insider trading. It emerged that Smith had made a profit of about £36,000 on the information provided, while Catherine Spearman had invested more than half a million pounds, netting over £100,000. Richard Spearman went for the chandeliers, investing over £2 million and making a profit approaching a quarter of a million pounds.

Michael David Smith of Loughton, Essex, pleaded guilty and was sentenced to 18 months' imprisonment, ordered to pay £36,012 by way of confiscation and to pay £50,000 towards the cost of the prosecution. He went to the Court of Appeal, where his sentence was upheld. Catherine Louise Spearman of Epping was also sentenced to 18 months' imprisonment, ordered to pay £107,935 by way of confiscation and to pay £50,000 towards the cost of the prosecution. She also went to the Court of Appeal, where the sentence was once again upheld. And Norman Payne of Epping received 30 months' imprisonment, though his sentence was later reduced to 21 months on appeal.

Only Richard Spearman pleaded not guilty, and went to trial by jury in January 2004. However, the jury was unable to reach a verdict, and a second trial was ordered. While on bail awaiting the retrial, Spearman was able to continue his business affairs unchecked. It proved a false dawn, however. Several months later, at Southwark Crown Court, Spearman was found guilty of conspiracy to commit insider dealing, sentenced to 30 months' imprisonment and ordered to pay £169,000 by way of compensation. Certainly as far as these insiders were concerned, their gamble on the Stock Exchange didn't pay off.

The Betting Exchange Conspiracies

I f horse racing is the sport of kings, and the Stock Exchange is the biggest casino in the world, then the newly formed internet online betting exchanges such as Betfair are the modern-day financial Wild West. Whenever sport and gambling go together, there is always the murky undercurrent of funny money, fixing, doping and downright skulduggery, especially when the outcome of an event can be predetermined – or at the very least when the odds can be tilted in the backer's favour, and the old enemy the bookmaker can be had over for a bundle. But, with the advent of the betting exchanges online, it is not necessarily the bookmaker who is the target any more. Because a player on a betting exchange can bet on the outcome of an event (or 'back', in old-fashioned betting parlance), he can now also bet *against* the outcome of an event (or 'lay'). Therefore, an exchange player with privileged or inside information can make a profit knowing about the outcome of an event that can't, or most likely won't, occur. Such a player can offer to lay the outcome of an event, often attractively at substantially over the odds, in the knowledge that a win is extremely unlikely, and is certainly not expected. He is therefore targeting the punter, or backer, and is playing the role of the bookmaker himself – and, in the context of horse racing, with the extra comfort of knowing that he has taken the bet on the unlikely winner and has all the other runners in the field running for him. Just in case.

Horse racing has been crooked for years, snooker has been framed by frame, darts is dodgy, tennis is tampered, boxing is bent and most other sports where large amounts of money are wagered on the results have been susceptible to manipulation, bribery and insider dealings. It is therefore unsurprising that, with the advent of betting exchanges, unusual betting patterns have emerged when crooked events are about to take place, and have been infiltrated by individuals and gangs of corrupt players who are in the know. While the actual idea of betting exchanges is really cool, the fact that they have agreed to a 'memorandum of understanding' with the Jockey Club and other sports' governing bodies lets the public know that they are aware of a problem.

Normally, a betting coup involves punters doing their utmost to have bookmakers over financially, target their overstuffed egos and collect a big pay day. This is normally achieved by the bettors having inside information about a potential winner, usually a horse, that they will go to any lengths to keep secret from the bookmakers, every person involved in the coup being on their word of honour to keep their plans a well-guarded secret until the event is over and the big payout has been received. Occasionally, the plan goes awry when a member of the syndicate gets a little chatty in a pub, or one of the conspirators gets too well acquainted with a bookmaker and changes sides, but normally these plans do work, albeit with less and less frequency now that bookmakers are wising up, and the online betting exchanges offer much more transparency in the betting jungle. The advent of the online betting exchanges, especially Betfair, has changed the market enormously.

In the old days, a punter would walk into a

licensed bookmakers and enquire about the price, or odds, on the outcome of an event. Say, for example, Tiger Woods was about to tee off for the Open. A potential Tiger Woods supporter walks into his local Ladbrokes: 'What price Woods for the Open?' he enquires.

'Four to one, sir,' the man dressed in the red waistcoat behind the counter replies.

'Four to bloody one? You're having a laugh!'

'Take it or leave it,' the Ladbrokes man replies, and the punter walks out, disgusted, with no room for negotiation.

In the local that evening, he gets chatting to his mates. 'Guess what price Woods is for the Open? Four to one, how skinny is that!'

His mates all agree. One chirps up, 'I'd lay him at fives, no question. Fives is fair – in fact, he should be eights, really.'

The next guy chips in, 'You can have 11–2 with me, only small, mind, I do fancy him a bit myself.'

And the original instigator of this conversation goes on to say, 'Well, if anyone wants to offer me sixes, I'm a punter!'

A couple of banknotes are passed across, hands are shaken, and two golf nuts with opposite views to the outcome can go and sit in front of the TV and enjoy the four days of play.

That is how the concept of betting exchanges was formed – punters all over the country, all over the world now, having an opinion on the outcome of an event. And many prepared to go against the outcome themselves, play bookie and take on the liability of the outcome at odds higher than is available in the high street from the likes of Messrs Ladbrokes and Co. It's understandable, too. Punters laying horses, football matches or golfers from the comfort of their homes don't have the expenses involved in running a chain of 2,000 licensed betting shops, and the associated overheads of rent, staff, insurance, advertising etc. – all of which, of course, has to be finally reflected in the reduced odds on offer. So it is easy to understand how a layer, taking an opinion on the outcome of an event, can be very easily persuaded to lay over the odds. And that is how Woods can be 6–1 on the betting exchanges online, while 4–1 in the bookies. And the beauty of the system is that you are guaranteed to get paid when you win, because Betfair simply act as a middleman matching the two bets for a commission. The punters are only able to back or lay an event if they have sufficient cleared funds in their Betfair account and, immediately the result is known, the loser is debited and the winner is credited, winnings that are readily accessible and can be drawn out at a moment's notice. No two-week accounting period with cheques in the post here.

Laying events to lose has obvious implications for the honesty and integrity of sport, and other events, however. A racehorse owner, in cahoots with a trainer, may decide to give their animal a quiet run on a particular race day for a variety of reasons. The horse may 'need the run' to improve for his next outing; the distance may be wrong, and a more suitable event not available for a few weeks; the competition may be too strong; or the price might be too short. For any of the above, or other reasons, or a combination of them, the horse may not be 'off', and the temptation to lay this horse on a betting exchange is almost irresistible. And, in a similar vein to the Tiger Woods scenario, exchange layers don't have the overheads and inconvenience of on-course bookmakers who have to travel to events, pay their entrance fees and taxes, hire staff to run their pitches, and play to a small percentage assuming every horse can win, and the event is straight. This plethora of connections of those 'in the know' includes the trainer, owner, jockey, blacksmith, stable lads and all the associates and friends connected with this string of individuals. So, when the horse you fancy goes off at an SP of 5–1 but is available at sevens online, be careful. You may be unwittingly backing an animal that has no chance of winning whatsoever.

Of course, a racehorse owner laying his horse to lose a race for a few quid will most likely get away with it. He could always argue, with conviction, that he was hedging his bets quite legitimately, anyway. If steam came on, he could maintain that he had only laid his horse to recoup sufficient money to cover his expenses of entering his horse into the race in the first place, and to cover his pocket money for his day out to watch his animal run. Had it won, he would have been delighted to pay the winning backer out of the euphoria of the win, and the prize money... However, there have been some more sinister coups landed on the betting exchanges, which go some way towards sullying the integrity of the sport of kings, and other, more obscure, off-the-wall events.

Betfair is the largest betting exchange in the world, with over 400,000 clients worldwide. It has received the Queen's Award for Enterprise, and is a very valuable business indeed. A stock-market flotation was mooted in July 2005, with Goldman Sachs and Morgan Stanley as advisors. The float valued Betfair at up to £700 million, and would have netted the two founders £100 million each. Although the stock-market deal didn't go ahead in the end, the betting exchange has signed a memorandum of understanding with the Jockey Club to preserve its integrity – an essential prerequisite for City standards of compliance. This memorandum requires the exchange to report any suspicious betting activity or patterns, such is the concern that players on the exchanges are getting involved in crooked races.

There have been recorded incidents, widely reported in the press, that have confirmed these fears. Five horses in particular caught the attention of Betfair security, bookmakers and the betting public in general: Royal Insult, Nimello, Hillside Girl, Hawk Flyer and Legal Set. Royal Insult drifted in price on the exchanges from 9–2 all the way out to 49–1, before breaking down at Lingfield after suffering a serious shoulder injury. Nimello was laid from 6–1 at all prices up to 32–1 before finishing lame at Salisbury, while Hillside Girl opening up at odds-on, ended up at an incredible 21–1 before pulling up after two furlongs. Hawk Flyer, meanwhile, was laid from 9–2 all the way out to 42–1 on Betfair for the St Ledger before pulling up lame on the gallops. And Legal Set, although not quite as dramatic a price move, attracted very substantial wagers when drifting from 9–4 to 4–1.

Another shining example of racehorse shenanigans concerned the story of a racehorse farrier who lost

£100,000 laying a horse on the exchanges. One wonders where that money came from. And then there have been the unusual betting patterns surrounding other horses that were deemed to be non-triers, and the huge amount of money that these were laid to on the exchanges, at well over the prevailing bookmakers' odds.

A further factor in the punters' favour on the exchanges is the ability to bet in running after the event is off. So, if your lay looks like winning, you can back it back during the course of an event to cover yourself. Nice work if you can get it! Then there are the obvious arbitrage opportunities. Many skilled players on the exchanges know in advance which events are likely to shorten in price before the off – known as 'steamers' in the trade – and which ones are going to go for a walk-in price and be friendless in the market. A trader armed with this information can quite easily back or lay something a couple of hours before the off, in the knowledge that he can then place the opposite trade later, when the odds have moved in his favour. And this type of arbitrage is not conducted for peanuts, either. A recent Premiership football match had over £1,500,000 matched before the match even kicked off. An average of £500,000 is bet on every horse race, and the exchange processes 12,000 bets a minute. Betting on football is massive business, especially when the outsiders score first and bookmakers are able to square up their books on the cheap.

Bookmakers are not averse to using the exchanges to hedge other bets, too. Quite perversely, the odds on offer for a horserace for the outsiders are enormously over the odds. Frequently, 33–1 shots are quoted at 66–1 or bigger, and, if an animal is priced up at 100–1 with the bookies, it could be as high as six or seven times that price on exchange. One wonders what kind of lunatics are prepared to bet £7,000 to win £70, but they do exist, and there have been some interesting tales of 1,000–1 shots coming in, skinning the layers who thought they were being so cool.

On one memorable occasion, Lady Luck deserted the layers as an astonishing series of events at Southwell left them out of pocket. In one of the most unusual races ever to take place on a British racetrack, all seven starters failed to put in a clear round in the 1.40. But the drama did not end there. Odds-on favourite Family Business was later remounted and steered to victory by champion jockey Tony McCoy. Hundreds of thousands of pounds had been staked in betting shops across Britain on the lucky winner. One Coral punter in West London waged a single bet of £5,000 only to walk out of the shop in disgust when McCoy's horse fell. He returned the following day to collect his winnings, gleaming! But, again, it was to be the betting exchange Betfair that stole the limelight on the event. When McCoy fell, one layer put up £4 at odds of 1,000–1 in running, someone matched it and the layer must have felt he had nicked his first beer for the day with the £4, and smiled at the stupidity of the punter who was backing the fallen mount with five horses still standing and running. But, unbelievably, all the five horses subsequently either fell, refused or unseated their rider. That prompted McCoy, the six-time champion jockey, to leap back on Family Business and enjoy an unchallenged ride to the finish line. This was, without question, one of the most extraordinary races ever seen, and is sure to feature on many pub quizzes for many years to come.

Two people were likely to have told and retold the tale in the pub that night: the layer who lost four grand trying to nick four quid, and the backer who cleaned up the four grand.

The champion jockey Tony McCoy couldn't believe his luck either. The scenes at Southwell were reminiscent of the 2001 Grand National, when only two horses completed the course unscathed, in heavy rain. On that occasion, McCoy again remounted, and ended up finishing third on Blowing Wind. Some bookmakers claimed the Southwell race should have been made void because Family Business had jumped one fence twice. However, steward's secretary Phil Tuck explained, 'We have spoken to London and they say that jumping a fence twice is not a reason for disqualification but it would be if he missed a fence out. A horse can be remounted and continue in the race as long as he goes back to where he departed.'

The standard time for the three miles one furlong test is 6 minutes 10.2 seconds. But, through all the mayhem, Family Business was timed at 10 minutes 30.9 seconds, including the spell while he was waiting for McCoy to renew their acquaintance.

Mark Bradburne, jockey on Oh No Whiskey, was taken to the Queen's Medical Centre in Nottingham to be 'checked over as a precautionary measure'. But the rest of the jockeys and horses escaped unscathed.

Huge payouts on Betfair are not just confined to horse racing and major sports. And rumours and speculation of skulduggery often abound. In December 2005, the Football Association launched a famous investigation into the massive £16.7 million worth of suspicious bets, which many considered to be a huge betting scam, placed at the time of Harry Redknapp's surprise return to Portsmouth from Southampton. Portsmouth Chairman Milan Mandaric and chief executive Peter Storrie were summonsed to an urgent meeting with the Football Association Compliance Department in London, after Betfair noticed a massive amount of money being staked on Redknapp just before Pompey confirmed he was to be their new manager. Betfair, under their new policy of complying with external investigations, not just on horse racing, even went to the lengths of supplying the FA print-outs of the bets that were placed, complete with a list of their clients' names, addresses and telephone numbers that accompanied it. The suspicion was that Redknapp, a man who is perfectly open about his gambling habits, might have leaked the information to those close to him, but the FA, after a long investigation, decided this was not the case, and the episode was closed – much to the relief of the footballing world.

Coincidentally, also in December 2005, a fraudulent gang pulled off a huge betting sting on Betfair that raked them in a fortune. A five-man team, all in their thirties, and who were very well educated (two having degrees from Leicester's De Montfort University) placed wagers on *X Factor*, *I'm a Celebrity…*, *Strictly Come Dancing* and *Big Brother*. They placed serious bets knowing they couldn't lose, because they knew the betting was corrupt. It turned out that these punters were being tipped off by text messages from a BT worker who had access to phone-vote totals for the programmes and passed on the winner's names to them just minutes before the results were announced live on the television. The team simply sat by their computers all over London and keyed in their bets straight to the betting exchanges, who simply continued to match their 'buyers and sellers'. Any bookmaker with common sense, seeing volumes of money on such obscure events, would immediately smell a rat, clip the price or more likely close his book there and then on the spot. The same team then went on to win more money on the outcome of reality shows like *Hell's Kitchen*, *The Farm*, *Hit Me One More Time* and *Celebrity Fame Academy*.

By now, they had scooped more than £100,000, an incredible sum on such events, and officials at Betfair became suspicious, for three main reasons. First, they had never witnessed such an incredible strike rate or run of luck on celebrity shows before. They were amazed at the size of the wagers for an event that was normally considered just to be a fun bet, and they were also concerned about the fact that the bets were consistently being placed literally minutes before the results were announced. Betfair suspected foul play, froze the remaining £45,000 that had not already been withdrawn from the gang's accounts and called in the police, a move they were not in the least bit hesitant to make to protect the integrity of their site and that of the other players who wager on it. The gang got tumbled, through their sheer greed and the telltale audit trail of unusual betting patterns.

Betfair have survived barrages of criticism and enquiry, though, and have continued to grow from strength to strength, recently expanding into Australia, with other horizons on their agenda. It seems that, despite the controversy, the betting exchanges are here to stay as the 21st-century way of conducting business in sport.

Just bear in mind that, the next time you log on and back or lay a result, you don't know who you are dealing with on the computer at the other end. The counterparty to your bet may be much closer to home than you would care to imagine.

11

The Financial Advisor With The £2.3 Million Gambling Habit

The top-of-the-range BMW pulled up outside the small sub-post-office branch in the quiet and leafy town of Bowdon, Manchester. Innocent people were going about their daily business – shopping, posting letters and collecting their pensions. The driver, Philip Smith, aged 49, was oblivious to everything around him and didn't seem to care that he had parked on double yellow lines. He casually got out of the luxury saloon and strolled into the post office, just as he had done every day for the previous 18 months. Smith looked every part the trusted businessman, dressed in a blue pinstripe suite, crisp white shirt, military tie and polished shoes. Once inside the post office, after the customary pleasantries were exchanged, he was handed a heavy bundle of letters by the postmistress, held together with a thick elastic band.

Smith eased himself back into his BMW and peeled open the bundle of letters he had been handed. The majority were in official cellophane wrappers and bore Royal Mail redirection stickers on them, because none of this mail was originally destined to be delivered to Philip Smith at all. It was mail he had secretly redirected to himself from many of his clients, because the contents of these letters revealed sinister material that Philip Smith, financial advisor, had to keep hidden from his clients at all costs. Most were credit-card statements and notifications of higher limits that had been redirected to him from all the clients who had lent him their cards to help him pay his 'office overheads'. He filed them all in the boot of the car. So how had Smith managed to con so many people out of so much money?

In the late 1980s, Philip Smith had worked as a financial advisor for the TSB bank in Stockport, a sleepy little town just outside Manchester. The county of Cheshire is home to some of the wealthiest people in the North, and Smith had a broad base of well-to-do customers to whom he gave financial advice under the TSB umbrella. By 1990, having by now come to appreciate how much commission was being raked in by the TSB, he realised that there was a huge potential in giving his advice as an independent financial advisor, and left the bank to set up in business on his own account. In those early days of regulation, registration as an independent financial advisor was quite a straightforward process, and with his banking background the authorities had no hesitation in granting Smith the authorisation and licences that he required.

Once set up in business, he began approaching his client base that he had built up at the TSB to tout for business, and to his delight many of his established clients left the newly appointed advisor at the bank and transferred their business and investments directly to his new investment outfit. The money started rolling in, and Smith enjoyed handling the large sums that he had under his auspices, some of which went into PIPs (personal investment plans), MIPs (monthly income plans), stocks and shares, the latest financial products that generated the largest introductory commissions – and, of course, his own little tickles and fancies.

Unfortunately for his clients, Philip Smith's tickles and fancies included spread betting on the outcome of sporting events and financial markets, and betting generally on sports such as horse racing and golf. To start with, Smith got lucky, dipping into his clients' accounts to borrow money to fund his gambling, and then using the winnings to replace what he had borrowed just as soon as his bookmaker's cheques had cleared. Soon he had credit accounts set up with a string of bookmakers, and every fortnight envelopes would arrive at his office containing statements from them – along with, more often than not during this golden period of backing winners, hefty cheques made out in the name of Philip Smith.

Then, quite suddenly, his run of luck came to an abrupt halt. Bookmakers have seen it all a million times before: the client who has umpteen winning weeks in a row, thinks he is invincible and ups the ante, believing foolishly that the settlement cheques will keep rolling in like manna from heaven, only to find he has squandered all the winnings, and more, in the matter of a few days. The bookies call it 'hitting the wall'. Out of form. Once Philip Smith hit the wall, a series of events were to unfold over a period of years that would leave him with a trail of angry victims, chaos and devastation, and facing court over one of the biggest financial crimes in Greater Manchester's history.

As soon as Philip Smith's money ran out – which, shockingly, happened over a period of only four days

– he turned his attention to the huge funds he had under his control from his investment clients. He believed that there must be a way that he could get his hands on some of this money – only for a few days of course, as a loan – to bail himself out of trouble with his gambling until his run of luck changed for the better.

The advent of internet gambling made life easy for Smith. Instead of having to put himself on offer first by turning up at banks demanding huge wads of cash, and then a second time by turning up at his bookies to place his bets in cash, online punting was secret, discreet and could be conducted on his laptop from the privacy of his office. So his mission in life now became to probe all his clients' accounts, see which had money in that was transferable to himself and get himself to work.

Many of Smith's clients were elderly, infirm or simply unsophisticated when it came to managing their finances. Quite a few had recommended their friends to Smith, too, and he was always able to coerce them into signing power of attorney forms so that he could have easy access to their funds. He would come up with plausible explanations for such a bizarre request by explaining that it was in their best interests as the markets moved so quickly, he needed to preserve their investments without contacting them. Discretion, if you like. Except that Philip Smith had a devious ulterior motive – he needed access to his clients' funds to fund his gambling, which was now very quickly spiralling out of control.

Within a matter of a few weeks, he had helped himself to sums that were well into six figures, money he found he quickly squandered on his online betting accounts, mainly by backing short-priced favourites at the races and luckless golfers. It was now time to up the ante – and help himself to even more money. Money he needed to prop up his ailing business, and keep him in the lifestyle to which he had become accustomed, as well, of course, as to fund his out-of-control gambling habit, which was now running into tens of thousands of pounds a day. Of course, sometimes he won, but he would persevere until it was all gone again. Every day he would sit in his office at his computer, and hit the browser to look at the current odds on offer from Betfair, Stan James, Blue Square and SpreadEx. With a click of the mouse, he would squander thousands, and put his investors' lives and retirements at risk.

Just as soon as he had got through the existing stash of money, an 88-year-old widow arrived at his office with a £150,000 investment policy. Smith persuaded her to deposit it with him, and, immediately she had done so, he managed to withdraw the entire £150,000 at once. This money went to finance another huge gambling orgy on the internet betting exchange Betfair, where Smith was racking up huge losses.

He then went on a wholesale crusade of plundering any account he could lay his hands on, and his modus operandi became even more cunning and daring. On at least one occasion, Smith telephoned a major financial institution and pretended to be someone who was actually dead to arrange for financial products to be surrendered. No client was safe. Smith took money from an elderly woman who had recently lost her husband, and siphoned off £82,000 that had been awarded to a man left unable to work after he was knocked down by a car.

To avoid detection, Smith arranged to have his victims' financial statements sent to his home address, so they did not find out what he was up to. Cleverly, he also allowed his registration with City regulators to lapse, leaving him totally unregulated. All of his clients were unaware of that, but he did it so that he wouldn't have to go through the process of annual checks, which would have meant the game was up, as by this time the legitimate accounts he kept were virtually non-existent. Instead, he set up a web of bogus investment information and falsified letters.

Naturally, when he came across an 87-year-old retired schoolteacher who had a massive savings account at the local building society, Smith became very interested in her. He managed to persuade her to set up a joint account with him at the building society, with Smith as a sole signatory. Over a short period of time, he stole £111,000 from the old dear.

Another victim whom he duped was Dilys Booth. She sought his services because he dealt with her aunt's financial affairs. On her aunt's death, Ms Booth asked him to invest her inheritance, but was conned out of £40,000. She admitted later that she could not believe how gullible she had been, explaining that Smith was very well thought of by many people, and that she had no idea he wasn't even registered.

While the bulk of all the stolen money was used to fund Smith's online gambling addiction, he also squandered a fortune on his lifestyle. He bought a home for £550,000 in Cheshire, a £170,000 villa on the Costa del Sol and a BMW 7 series. He even had the audacity to invite his clients to stay at his villa in Spain free of charge – if only they'd known that they had paid for it!

When his clients' investment accounts were bled dry, and he had precious little left in his online gambling accounts to fund his addiction, Smith thought up a new ploy to fund his punting. He drove round to see all of his clients, and told them how well all their investments were doing. At the same time, he asked if he could borrow their credit cards to help pay his office running expenses. Unbelievably, they all agreed, and Smith started secretly using the credit cards to deposit money into his various online betting accounts.

Click-click on the mouse, lose-lose on the screen – oops! Another good idea required to keep the ball rolling! Now Smith contacted the credit-card companies, and upped the limits on all the cards without the owners knowing. Desperate to avoid detection, he now redirected all the credit-card statements to the small local sub-post office in Bowdon. He was amazed at how long he had got away with his scams – almost ten years so far, and not a single squeal from any of his clients; it was as if they were all asleep. He didn't have to worry about any spot checks or audits from the regulators, either, as he was no longer regulated.

Smith's undoing was to come from a source that he would least expect. A fraud investigator at the building society where he had set up the joint account became suspicious of the large number of withdrawals, involving a substantial sum of money, that had taken place over a short period of time, and began an investigation. When it transpired that all of the money had been credited to online betting accounts, the police were called in and were actually speaking to one of Smith's elderly victims when the man himself turned up at her house for an appointment, intending to relieve her of even more money. A search of his car revealed hundreds of documents.

A massive police investigation followed, which revealed that at one stage Smith had operated 14 accounts with a single bookmaker, and had a total of 67 credit and debit cards registered with them – only a handful of which were in his own name. He was also using a further ninety cards to set up online betting accounts. Through these accounts, he gambled £2 million. He used the winnings to buy his properties and maintain his lifestyle, while the losses were simply dumped on to the innocent cardholder's account, debit statements of which Smith filed in his car boot.

In September 2006, Philip Smith pleaded guilty to a raft of offences including theft, forgery and money laundering when he appeared at Minshull Street Crown Court in Manchester. He admitted stealing

£1.75 million and laundering a further £600,000 from at least 51 clients.

Detective Constable John Ashington, from Stockport CID, later commented, 'Philip Smith was a man driven by greed, selfishness and ultimately desperation. He has left not only financial chaos and devastation in his wake, but also dozens of decent and hard-working people feeling shocked, shattered, betrayed and angry. Some have started to suffer health problems when they discovered what Smith had done. Gathering the evidence to bring Smith to justice has been a long and challenging task. But this man has left dozens of honest people in terrible financial difficulties. People who were looking forward to a comfortable retirement now face worry and uncertainty.

'Theft and deception on such a large scale is very rare. I have seen at first hand the misery and distress that Smith has caused and I sincerely hope that I do not have to deal with another case like this ever again. Ultimately, I hope that something good can come out of this case and that people will look to take extra care when deciding how to invest their money. As this case has shown, even if an independent financial advisor is recommended by a friend or member of family, it's important to check with the FSA that they are bona fide and fully registered.'

Judge Peter Lakin told Smith, 'This is a very serious case with a number of aggravating factors. You must understand, as I'm sure you do, that you have pleaded guilty to very serious matters and that the court is bound to have in mind a substantial custodial sentence.'

One wonders what spread Philip Smith would have bet on the prison sentence he would receive. In the end, it turned out to be nine years.

Cheating At Poker

Some years ago, there was a TV discussion about the coverage of competitive sport, and a survey of which sports the viewing public most enjoyed watching. It was one of those old-fashioned programmes where four experts were sitting on a couch in front of the cameras in the studio late on a Saturday night, going through the pros and cons of televised basketball, ping pong, darts and snooker. All of a sudden, one of the less geriatric members of the team blurted out that poker was a competitive sport but that, of course, we would never see it on television. He was obviously a card aficionado, but the studio went silent, the mere mention of the game of poker seeming to besmirch the integrity of the BBC.

In those days, the image of poker was that of a game played for large bundles of cash by East End villains in a smoky basement, with the liquor flowing as freely as the bad language, and heavies at the door. If you were foolish enough to get involved in such a game, and you were lucky enough to win, you would be even luckier to leave intact with your ill-gotten gains. In those days, no one could have imagined poker becoming a popular televised commodity, being played all over the world for millions of dollars. Its image was simply too nefarious. However, the viewing public tend to believe that what they see on the television, and hear on the radio, is true – properly researched and monitored, and transmitted clean as a whistle. Ask any convicted con artist which media would be his choice of self-promotion, and the TV and radio will tie for first place. The general public, in their naivety, have also been led to believe that, if a sport is televised, it is being run according to honest rules of engagement and properly supervised to avoid the chance of cheating. Nothing could be further from the truth – especially as far as televised poker is concerned.

Poker has always had the image of a low-life game, practised by players of – shall we say – a dubious background. It was essential that, in order to imbue the game with a presentable image for worldwide television, some of the taboos and myths surrounding it would have to be swept to one side. The introduction of the TV-friendly 'Texas Hold'em' version of poker improved the marketability of the game, certainly as far as the TV cameras were concerned; the venues and the style of the competitions, many being played for enormous prize pools by branded players, completed the scenario. The advent of internet poker helped to cement the magic illusion, with entries to these fabulous events available online. Many winners of large prizes had qualified on internet poker sites, for a pittance, which provided a great background story for journalists. The scene was set for a fantastic marketing and broadcasting coup, and today one can hardly turn on Sky TV late at night without finding coverage of a poker game somewhere. However, clever cardsharps and poker old-timers were to prove themselves streets ahead of the tournament organisers and TV directors when it came to stacking the odds in their favour in their quest to get their hands on the enormous prize money on offer.

In the 2006 World Series of Poker (WSOP) in Las Vegas, the winner, Jamie Gold, received a prize cheque of $12 million. That's much, much more than

Tiger Woods got for winning the Open recently. Although entry to the World Series cost $10,000, many of the internet poker sites offered incentives and free entries, which made the event more glamorous and marketable – witness the plethora of branded T-shirts and baseball caps. Online poker sites are now even sponsoring film channels. The WSOP is not just about the main multi-million-dollar event, though. There are numerous other high-value competitions that precede it, and many budding poker players from all over the world are keen to take their chances in as many games as possible, for the tantalising possibility of playing against one of the greats, and often making a poker trip to Vegas last for several weeks. However, there is a dark side to the game of tournament poker, even at the World Series level. For the game is rampant with cheating.

Seasoned poker professionals acknowledge that the difference in the standard of play between themselves and an amateur – say, one who has been playing online for a year or so – is maybe only 2 or 3 per cent. That is one of the attractions of the game: an unknown novice can beat one of the best in the world, given a modicum of luck and some skill, in complete contrast to other games of skill, such as chess or backgammon. That is why thousands of hopeful poker players flock to their favourite internet sites and try to qualify for big events such as the World Series, winning satellites in massive fields of hundreds of players to avoid having to stump up the $10,000 entry fee. Some of the poker sites even offer competitions in which the winner receives free travel, hotel and pocket money as well, a fabulous incentive. Recently, Chris Moneymaker won the World Series after qualifying online for a mere $40. He immediately became a (highly marketable) legend in the poker world. The oddest thing about the game of poker at this high level, however, is that the same players seem to keep reaching the final tables, again and again, year after year, with many ordinary players consistently dropping out in the early stages of the tournament. Can this really just be a case of skill and experience triumphing over less experienced novice players? I think not.

To reach the final table in a tournament takes a considerable run of consistent good fortune and skill, often over many days and long hours of play, and in the process you have to win many coin flips during all-in situations. Once you have survived this onslaught, sometimes over a period of several days' play on many different tables against many different players, you have to go through the whole process again on the final table of nine players itself. Given the odds of winning all the coin flips, and the aforementioned small skill differentials between the top and novice players, there has been suspicion, to say the very least, that all is not quite as it seems in the poker world. Some players have even reached the final tables at spectacles such as the WSOP in several different tournaments in the same year, collecting enormous sums of prize money for their efforts. They must be excellent players, surely... or do they have a hidden secret weapon and agenda? Of course they do, and I am now going to blow the lid off what *really* goes on behind the scenes of poker tournaments, at the highest level of play, all over the world.

The first thing to appreciate about major poker tournaments is that the leading contestants who make it big time and appear to be winning huge amounts of money actually only own a very small percentage of it themselves, so by the time that they slog it out to the final table their prize fund has been greatly diminished. However, they will have at the same time taken a share or interest in some of their fellow players too, creating a situation in which a certain group of players have a large vested financial interest in themselves as a team, and will go to any lengths to ensure their survival through the ranks. The set-up of players investing in other players whom they are playing against will always happen at major poker tournaments. When entry fees to some competitions are as high as $10,000 or more a go, this is sometimes the only way some of these players can afford to participate in the first place. In some tournaments, some players might have a piece of the action in as many as forty or fifty players, so it is easy to understand how they have a vested interest in reaching the prize-money stages. And, if you analyse the prize structure, you can understand why. Consider 8,500 players put up $10,000 each in entry-fee money. That creates a prize pool of $85 million. The way the prize pool is structured, with $12 million going to the winner, and prize money all the way down to 500th place, the odds of winning the competition are severely diminished. Plus, the organisers will have raked off a decent percentage from the top of the pot, to cover their expenses, and a profit. Obviously, this means that less money is being paid out than has been paid in. And this means that the top players, in order to obtain value, have no choice but to gang up together and agree to play as a team, at the expense of the hapless no-hopers who are going to get burned out of the competition early, and forfeit all those $10,000 buy-ins to the master syndicate. Put simply, this is collusion in its purest form, and it is rife at high-level tournament poker.

This is how it works. Six well-known players –

perhaps professionals who battle it out week after week at the poker tables in tournaments all over the world and know each other well – meet up a few days before a tournament is about to begin and agree to play, effectively, as a team. The financial benefits to them are enormous. These players are not after the glory of being televised on the final table in showdowns; although they undoubtedly have large egos, they are far more interested in winning cash. And, by working together, they are stacking the odds tremendously in their favour. Say a smaller event than the World Championship costs $2,500 to enter, and the prize pool is $200,000; playing as a group gives the syndicate far more chance of hitting the jackpot than if they all played solo. So they agree to help each other out, three of the team members being designated as suppliers, and the other three as receivers. The supplier's role is to provide his chips to the receiver, normally in a 'heads-up' situation, to enhance his stack to such an extent that it will make a material difference to his game. As tournaments progress, and the small-blind/big-blind antes go up, short-stacked players become increasingly unlikely to win. It is therefore imperative that at least one member of the team moves through the ranks to the next table with a substantial stack of chips, in order to give him a fair crack of the whip. And the other players in the collusion team are quite happy to sacrifice their chips to one of their team-mates at crucial times of the tournament to assist him in having a fair crack at making the final table – which, of course, would provide a pay day for the entire team.

This form of cheating is known as 'chip dumping' and is strictly speaking illegal in poker, but it happens all the time. I have watched hours of video recordings of major poker tournaments and have found evidence of chip dumping, at the highest levels, between many well-known players. Year after year, the same players are involved in this practice. A certain number of these high-class players have reached the final tables so many times that you could be forgiven for thinking that they had entered the competition at the very last moment with a huge pile of chips, and had only to play a couple of hands before moving straight to the final table. So how does the scam work?

Our six friends are intent on the three receivers building up their stacks of chips, to give them the maximum chance when they are approaching the final. As soon as two of the team make the same table, it is the job of the supplier to give up his chips to the receiver at the least obvious but most appropriate opportunity. As soon as he is in a suitable position on the table vis-à-vis the blind structure, the receiver will be looking for an opportunity to go into a 'heads-up' battle with the provider. Through the use of sophisticated prearranged signalling, the two players discover what each other's hole cards are. This is done by placing their chips as card guards on their hands: the exact position of the chips determines the value of the hand. Top left corner A-A, top middle K-K, top right Q-Q, left centre J-J, middle centre 10-10, right centre 9-9 and so on and so forth. This clever strategy of using chips and cards to signal to one's cohorts the value of pocket cards is almost foolproof, and the team are very careful not to use signalling devices that involve the face or fingers – certainly not for indicating the value of their hands. But they also practise discreet physical signals, such as scratching the nose, rubbing the chin and pulling on the earlobe to indicate other scenarios, such as when they want the all-in call.

Signalling was a little more difficult for high hands that were not pairs, but the scammers found a way around this, too, by using two chips as card guards to give away the secret. What the duo are looking for is the receiver with a strong hand, and the supplier with a strongish one – although the supplier's hand is not that important, as we will see shortly. The receiver has to quickly add up the number of chips held by the supplier, because this is going to determine the size of his raise. Given a weak betting hand, the receiver will make a large raise, and the supplier will call, to within a whisker of his chip stack. The rest of the table folds, and the pair now see the entire five community cards dealt, having checked throughout. If by the river the receiver knows he has a winning hand, he will put the supplier all-in, they will show their hands and he will be the next one out of the competition, to much commiseration from the other players at the table. If, however, the supplier has fluked the winning hand, he will simply fold his hand, and acknowledge the receiver's 'winning hand'. Whichever method, the result is the same, and the receiver has built up his chip stack nicely, ready to take on the rest of the players on his behalf, and on behalf of the rest of his cohorts.

As competitions draw closer and closer to the holy grail of the final table of nine and the alluring prize money, more and more players are knocked out. This sometimes goes in spurts and runs, especially when three players are involved in a showdown, when two may be eliminated at once. Tournament organisers are always keen to have their tables evenly balanced, so players are moved frequently from table to table to keep them full at all times.

Sometimes, three of the cohorts end up playing on the same table together, and that is when the real fun begins: the other seven players have no idea of the shock they are about to receive. When the conspirators end up three to a table, their modus operandi changes, and the collusion team's bad hands protect its good ones. The bad hands have a function, which is to draw extra chips into the pot when the cohorts' hand is very strong. Members of the cheating team with bad hands play a very important role in raising their bet when it is their turn to act, generating more chips in the pot for their accomplice with the strong hand, and then simply folding at the appropriate time so as to avoid suspicion. A cheating team of three can thus manipulate the betting structure on the table, rope in their unsuspecting challengers into the net, and more than likely win pots with their bully tactics, even if they do not have the best hand. Should one of the team actually have the nuts – three times more likely than a single player, if you think about it – then, again, the maximum can be drawn from the rest of the field. In this way, the cohorts have a very strong chance indeed of getting one of their team through to the next table, high on adrenalin, chips and betting power, ready to take on the rest of the players with his secret ammunition of collusion and betting power with his ill-gotten chips. And, once the field has dwindled down to the vital last couple of tables, the big collusive moves of chip-dumping are executed.

While using chips are the preferred method of signalling hole cards to the other team members, there are other methods used too. Sophisticated players sometimes 'finger' their cards on the table, tapping their cards on the correct spot to identify their value. I have seen both these methods used frequently, and would consider them both to be very effective and almost undetectable. As the great casino cheat Joe Classon once said, 'Never leave any evidence behind when you are operating a scam.'

There is a third method, though, which is also ingenious. Most players at poker tables handle and shuffle their chips while waiting for their next move, with some having perfected clever tricks with their chips and elaborate shuffles. Some of these 'must-have' chip-shuffling techniques are even available for sale on the internet. Needless to say, some mechanics and cheats have elaborated a way to shuffle their chips in a certain manner and with specific stacks and denominations to signal their hands to their accomplices. And then there is the verbal collusion. Once a predetermined verbal code has been agreed upon, a simple question about the weather, the last hand, the ball game or the lottery result can have sinister implications for the other players.

Despite the shrewd advice of the legendary Joe Classon, cheating involving the marking of cards is also evident in poker, although it is much less common than collusion. At the 2006 WSOP, which had a record number of entries, the first few days degenerated into a state of chaos, with dealers threatening to walk out over a pay dispute and players complaining bitterly about the quality of the decks being dealt, many for two or three days at a time. There was strong evidence of card marking, attained by putting tiny creases or crimps, or even little nail scratches on the back of face cards.

In fact, a new and highly sophisticated card-marking scam took America by storm recently, one so ingenious that it must surely rank as the ultimate card-marking story ever. An optometrist discovered a colourless liquid that could mark cards in a way that could only be detected by someone wearing a specially designed pair of contact lenses. The beauty of this product was that it was odourless, and it disappeared without a trace after 30 minutes. The problem was how to get the solution on to the backs of the cards during play. One team found the perfect method. A glamorous lady team member kept the solution in her make-up bag, and, from time to time, as all ladies do, she would remove her compact at the card table to powder her nose, and at the same time apply a few drops of the solution to her fingers, undetected. She was then able to mark her cards over a few hands, giving her and the rest of her team a serious advantage over the rest of the unsuspecting players, and enabling the team to clean up, literally. Joe Classon would have approved.

Card-switching is another method of cheating at poker. Clever mechanics can swap a hole card with a partner sitting next to them. Imagine being dealt King-three, with your partner receiving King-six. A quick mechanic team would be able to swap the three for the King, giving him a monster starting pair. These mechanics perfect their acts so the switch goes completely unnoticed, and happens in literally a split second, well disguised with their arms, which are placed at such an angle as to prevent anyone noticing, and ostensibly to protect their own cards from prying eyes!

Dealers are not averse to getting in on bent poker action too, often teaming up with a player at their table in a conspiracy to cut the profits. A slick dealer can keep high cards together in a clump during a fake shuffle, deal his partner a monster hand, and then secretly show – by undetectable and subtle thumb and finger signals – when to check, call, raise or fold.

A dealer–player collusion syndicate is probably one of the most powerful moves in poker cheating; it is very profitable, impossible to beat and is extremely difficult to spot. Stealing money at poker is almost the ultimate financial crime, because the advantage is that no money is missing after it has been stolen.

Internet poker is riddled with cheats. Put simply, the integrity of a significant number of the online poker sites sucks. Collusion online is easy, and the poker sites are aware of it. Furthermore, there are computer hackers out there who have devised extremely clever and sophisticated software to enable them to actually see their opponents' hole cards. And some players don't trust the honesty of the sites themselves. Many of the online poker businesses were started up by entrepreneurs with, shall we say, dubious track records.

In order to appreciate how vulnerable the actual games of poker offered by these online sites are, one has to look at the software used by these firms. Online poker is dealt by the use of shuffles and deals generated by the use of random number generators. However, these programs are not idiot proof, and a few years ago a group of computer programmers found a gaping black hole in online card-room security. They discovered a means of precisely calculating the order of cards that were to be dealt from a shoe at poker, enabling them to know what every player's hole cards were, and also the order of cards that were to be dealt for the flop, turn and river. The algorithm that was the starting point for the deal was programmed to the number of milliseconds past midnight according to the system's clock. All the card-cheating computer gurus had to do was synchronise their program with the computer clock, and they were on to winning without any risk. Online card rooms insist that this trapdoor has now been firmly shut, but I for one am certain that computer experts will find another one soon.

As with live poker games, however, collusion is a much more sinister problem, and online poker sites employ full-time security to stamp it out. However, their ammunition is plainly inadequate, and mainly revolves around checking the IDs, computer addresses and credit-card details of players who frequently play on the same tables. The inference is obvious: a team from the same town playing on the same online table, could actually be huddled round a live dining table in one of the team member's houses with half a dozen laptops on the go – or, more likely, be disclosing their hands to one another via SMS messages or mobile-phone calls themselves. The poker site security departments are very quick to claim that they shut down such players, but fail to admit that sophisticated cheats are going to simply bypass this obvious system and go to much greater lengths of setting up IDs in different cities, with the use of multiple credit cards, different log-in IDs and much more. From experience, I would estimate that 5 per cent of the online poker games are infiltrated by players who are in collusion with each other. Colluders are always trying to find newer and safer methods of beating the sites, and the stakes they are playing for are high, many millions of pounds changing hands online every day. But they have to be careful, too. If caught, they face being barred from the site, and they also run the risk of having their account balances frozen at the same time.

The most dramatic method of online cheating at poker has to be the ultimate software program, which is available to those in the know. It is expensive, but is worth every penny, and is called 'Peeker'. This incredible computer program – obviously only available on the black market, and only offered to the most trusted players – actually lets you see the other players' hole cards while playing online poker from the comfort of your own home.

Wonders will never cease in the hi-tech gadgetry surrounding online gaming, so the next time you sit down at a poker table, be it live or online, be aware that there are forces surrounding you that may not all be legitimate. You could be playing live against colluders, or online against robots.

The Nigerian '419' Advance Fee Scam

Nigeria – officially, the Federal Republic of Nigeria – is a West African country with the largest population of any nation on the African continent. The Nigerian state officially came into being on 1 October 1960, when the country declared its independence from Great Britain. It comprises 36 states and the federal capital territory. In 1999, democracy returned to the country after a series of military dictatorships.

Nigeria is infamous for its corruption and fraud. Scammers abound in their thousands, and very few Westerners have ever managed to succeed in legitimate business in this African country, such is the level of corruption that goes right to the very heart of government, policing, judiciary and commerce. Scammers in Nigeria can draw on a massive armoury of weapons to assist them in their quest of relieving Westerners of large sums of money. Because the country is so corrupt, it is easy for the scammers to bribe government officials to lend them impressive-looking letterheads to send out faxes and letters; government seals are brokered on the cheap; and officials themselves are happy to participate in a potential fraud by lending themselves, their office or business premises and their colleagues to the fraudsters – always for a fee, of course. The police, customs and immigration officials are not shy to get in on the act also, so any poor visitor to Nigeria really does have a battle on his hands.

Recently, a team of Nigerian scammers touted some vials of gold grain around the bullion dealers in Hatton Garden, London. The gold was of incredible purity and worth a lot of money – at least £250 an ounce. The Nigerians, posing as government officials, simply walked round Hatton Garden, and left samples of the gold with each of the bullion dealers, plus an impressive-looking business card, complete with crests, logos and phone and fax numbers. Their colleagues in Nigeria were waiting by the phones to act out the part should anyone in London phone to check up the authenticity of what was claimed. Two greedy and naive bullion dealers were had. They were persuaded that they could have access to tonnes of this gold, at a very attractive price, but were told they would have to travel to Nigeria to put down a deposit of £40,000 in cash to guarantee them the deal. Neither had any hesitation in doing so, and the scammers very cleverly arranged for the two bullion dealers to arrive in Nigeria on the same day, but on different flights.

All went well until the first dealer arrived at the airport. Here he was met by four 'customs officials' in uniforms, who took him to a room to have his luggage examined and to be searched. When they found the £40,000 in cash, they took it from him, explaining that they were going to a senior officer's department to process the money, that the visitor should sit tight as it could take a while to obtain the necessary authorisation for him to enter the country with such a large sum, and that all the banknotes would have to be examined and the serial numbers on the notes would all have to be recorded. Then, they simply locked him in the room, disappeared with his money and waited for the second bullion dealer to arrive. When he turned up, the same procedure was repeated by the four scammers, who took him to a different room, which they had also bribed an officer to let them use, removed his money and locked him in there too, before making their getaway. It took the bullion dealers, both of whom were astute operators in the metals markets, five hours to realise what had happened to them and to get themselves released from their temporary prisons. The hapless two then had to sit around and wait for the next flight back to the UK, eighty grand lighter.

Lawyers, accountants, leaders of industry and businessmen all over the world have fallen prey to such scams, often referred to as 'front fee fraud', 'the Nigerian fortune scam' or simply as '419', as this is the section of the Nigerian law dealing with fraud. The reason so many astute businessmen fall for the scam is painfully simple: the Nigerians are clever at exploiting people's greed. Despite warnings about the '419' scam, on websites, in publications all over the world and by word of mouth, it continues to flourish with alarming regularity, and it has even been suggested that it is the third to fifth largest industry in Nigeria. In the United States, a popular location for the Nigerian fraudsters to target, the authorities receive over a hundred phone calls and around five hundred pieces of written information about this scam on a daily basis, and it is estimated that the fraud brings in hundreds of millions of dollars a year. With such a golden egg to protect, it is little surprise that the corrupt members of government in Nigeria are in on it, and many were in fact scammers themselves before being appointed as government officials. It is of little surprise, therefore, that money stolen from victims in this type of scam is hardly ever recovered from Nigeria, and victims have little or no recourse. No doubt because international communications are today much simpler since the advent of the internet, the scam has widened its horizons and has recently been seen in Southeast Asia, Russia and New Zealand, but, whatever the destination of the scam, one can be assured that the source is always Nigeria.

Victims of the '419' scam typically receive a letter or an email purporting to be from someone in a position of power and trust in Nigeria who has come into a huge sum of money and needs a foreign bank account to get it out of the country. In the old days, these letters were sent out by hand from Lagos, sometimes in their millions a week, but, with the advent of the internet, they are normally now bulk-emailed to mailing lists which are purchased by the scammers. And there is reportedly evidence that the Nigerian government themselves are involved in the scam, too.

Scammers often present themselves as high officials of the Central Bank of Nigeria. Investigators of '419' fraud all over the world have been able to ask for by name and speak with the scammers at the Central Bank of Nigeria – the phone number for the bank being obtained from Lagos directory enquiries and not from the scammers themselves. It is no wonder that victims have difficulty in recovering money lost in the scam.

Another take on the '419' scam works like this. The Nigerian scammers announce that they have this enormous sum of money to get out of their country. Plausible explanations are given as to the source of the money. These include stories about ministers having being killed in plane crashes, with untold millions in bank accounts that are about to be confiscated by the Nigerian government in a matter of days if it isn't transferred abroad, and oil and weapons money that is also at risk if not moved quickly; urgency is always a hallmark of the scam. The ultimate aim of the scammers is to secure details of the victim's bank account. They obtain the bank details with the promise of the millions being transferred into it, and the enticement of a large percentage as a commission. However, once the scammers have details of the bank account, it is plundered. Sometimes the scam is drawn out over a period of weeks, with the victims being asked to send upfront payments (advance fee fraud) for expenses before the money is transferred. Some victims have been known to send multiple payments, often amounting to tens of thousands of dollars, before realising they have been had. Victims who fly to Lagos to hand over their fees sometimes disappear without trace. And anyone who dares to prosecute or challenge the Nigerians normally meets a sticky end.

Here is a sample of the kind of '419' letter a victim may receive. (Note: The letter that is sent is nearly always in capital letters, and contains many grammatical and spelling mistakes.)

LAGOS, NIGERIA.

ATTENTION: THE PRESIDENT/CEO

DEAR SIR,

CONFIDENTIAL BUSINESS PROPOSAL

HAVING CONSULTED WITH MY COLLEAGUES AND BASED ON THE INFORMATION GATHERED FROM THE NIGERIAN CHAMBERS OF COMMERCE AND INDUSTRY, I HAVE THE PRIVILEGE TO REQUEST FOR YOUR ASSISTANCE TO TRANSFER THE SUM

OF $47,500,000.00 (FORTY SEVEN MILLION, FIVE HUNDRED THOUSAND UNITED STATES DOLLARS) INTO YOUR ACCOUNTS. THE ABOVE SUM RESULTED FROM AN OVER-INVOICED CONTRACT, EXECUTED, COMMISSIONED AND PAID FOR ABOUT FIVE YEARS (5) AGO BY A FOREIGN CONTRACTOR. THIS ACTION WAS HOWEVER INTENTIONAL AND SINCE THEN THE FUND HAS BEEN IN A SUSPENSE ACCOUNT AT THE CENTRAL BANK OF NIGERIA APEX BANK.

WE ARE NOW READY TO TRANSFER THE FUND OVERSEAS AND THAT IS WHERE YOU COME IN. IT IS IMPORTANT TO INFORM YOU THAT AS CIVIL SERVANTS, WE ARE FORBIDDEN TO OPERATE A FOREIGN ACCOUNT; THAT IS WHY WE REQUIRE YOUR ASSISTANCE. THE TOTAL SUM WILL BE SHARED AS FOLLOWS: 70% FOR US, 25% FOR YOU AND 5% FOR LOCAL AND INTERNATIONAL EXPENSES INCIDENT TO THE TRANSFER.

THE TRANSFER IS RISK FREE ON BOTH SIDES. I AM AN ACCOUNTANT WITH THE NIGERIAN NATIONAL PETROLEUM CORPORATION (NNPC). IF YOU FIND THIS PROPOSAL ACCEPTABLE, WE SHALL REQUIRE THE FOLLOWING DOCUMENTS:

(A) YOUR BANKER'S NAME, TELEPHONE, ACCOUNT AND FAX NUMBERS.

(B) YOUR PRIVATE TELEPHONE AND FAX NUMBERS – FOR CONFIDENTIALITY AND EASY COMMUNICATION.

(C) YOUR LETTER-HEADED PAPER STAMPED AND SIGNED.

ALTERNATIVELY WE WILL FURNISH YOU WITH THE TEXT OF WHAT TO TYPE INTO YOUR LETTER-HEADED PAPER, ALONG WITH A BREAKDOWN EXPLAINING, COMPREHENSIVELY WHAT WE REQUIRE OF YOU. THE BUSINESS WILL TAKE US THIRTY (30) WORKING DAYS TO ACCOMPLISH.

PLEASE REPLY URGENTLY.

BEST REGARDS

Nigerian fraud letters are not just related to this particular scam. One of the more sinister (but almost amusing) frauds involves the 'Black Money' scam. In this ruse, the victim is shown a suitcase of 'money' that had been dyed black, so it could be got out of the country. The Nigerian conmen would then produce one of the black notes, apply a special chemical to it, or put it through a special roller, and – hey presto – a real $100 bill. The victim would then part with a very substantial sum of money for the special chemical or roller, only to find, of course, that when he applied it to the suitcase of black banknotes... he had been sold a suitcase of black paper cut out to resemble banknotes.

Be very careful if you ever receive such letters, either in the post or by email. The best advice if you ever receive any such correspondence is to file them in your rubbish bin.

As a happier footnote on which to end, one British man is actually fighting the Nigerian fraudsters at their own game. Mike Berry goes along with the scammers and baits them by demanding that they send photos of themselves bearing codewords on large pieces of cardboard held out in front of themselves. The codewords normally run along the lines of 'plonker'. He also tells the fraudsters to fly to meetings to which he never turns up. He has received death threats, but hopes that by wasting the scammers' time he is stopping them from targeting other victims.

Glossary Of Gambling Terms

ACTION – Any kind of wager.

ALL-IN – In poker, if a player runs out of money during a hand, he can play out the hand, but he's excluded from betting in the remaining rounds. When this happens the player is 'all-in'. The other players continue betting in a side pot, which excludes the all-in player. If the all-in player wins the hand, he gets the money in the original pot, but the money in the side pot goes to the remaining player with the best hand.

ALLOWANCE RACE – Horses in allowance races must meet certain conditions to run. The amount of weight carried by a horse in such a race is based on the number of races the horse has run and the amount of money it has won.

AMERICAN WHEEL – A roulette wheel with a total of 38 numbers (0, 00, and numbers 1 to 36).

ANTE – When poker players place a small bet into the pot before the hand starts. Antes ensure that there is at least a small amount of money invested in a game before everyone can fold.

ANTE-POST – A bet made well before the event, when the odds are usually more favourable.

ARBITRAGE – An investment where the profit is made on the margin when the same item is priced differently on two exchanges or in different bookies' odds.

BACCARAT – A card game in which two or more punters back against the dealer.

BACKGAMMON – A board game for two players in which the pieces' moves are determined by throws of the dice.

BAD BEAT – A good hand is beaten by a long shot.

BANKROLL – Money available to a person making a bet.

BASIC STRATEGY – Using the plays in blackjack that enable you to maximise your chances of winning.

BELLYBUSTER – An inside straight draw in which only one card will make the hand. If you have 5-6-8-9, you have one bellybuster because you need a 7 to complete the straight. Also referred to as a 'gutshot'.

BEST OF IT – To have 'the best of it' means you got your money into the pot while the odds were in your favour. You might still lose the hand, but that's just a matter of luck. Top players don't worry about winning as much as getting their money in with 'the best of it' more often than not.

BETFAIR – The biggest of the internet betting exchanges. Betfair was formed in 2000 and enables its clients to bet with one another, thus eliminating the need for a bookie.

BIAS – When a horse is more likely to win if it runs

on one part of the running surface rather than on another part.

BINGO CARD – The card used for playing Bingo. It contains five rows and five columns of boxes with the letters 'B I N G O' printed across the top. Winning at Bingo entails forming required patterns by filling boxes as their corresponding numbers are called.

BLANK – A useless card.

BLIND BET – In poker, a blind bet is a bet that selected players are required by the rules to make. It serves the same purpose as an ante.

BLUFFING – A poker player is bluffing when he bets and raises in an effort to make his opponents believe his hand is better than it really is.

BOOKMAKER (or BOOKIE) – A person who lays odds on the result of any future event, but most commonly horses and sports. The bookie offers odds against all the runners or outcomes and maintains a book, keeping a record of his liability in any race as each wager is taken.

BRING-IN – A bring-in is when a poker player is

forced to get the betting started by opening with a minimum bet. The bring-in bet serves as an ante for seven-card games. It's made after all the players have been dealt their first up-card. The player with the lowest showing card gets the honours. The second bettor can match the bring-in, raise to the minimum bet level or fold.

BUST – Going over 21 in blackjack. If you bust, you lose.

BUST OUT – To get eliminated from a tournament by losing all your chips.

BUTTON – This is a small marker in poker that's moved from player to player after each hand to designate the dealer position. The designated dealer position is shifted from hand to hand to ensure that each player is required to take his turn putting up blind bets. The button is moved clockwise around the table after each hand.

BUY-IN – The amount of money you need to put up in order to play in a game or enter a tournament.

CALLER – The person who calls out the numbers in a Bingo game as they are drawn.

CALLING – In poker, this is when a player matches a previous bet.

CALLING STATION – Derisive term for a weak player who often calls other players' bets but rarely raises or initiates action.

CARD COUNTER – A blackjack player who tracks the cards that have been dealt, in order to know which cards remain in the deck. In this way, card counters can work out when they are most likely to beat the dealer – at which point they will make their largest bets.

CARD GUARD – A small round gaming chip or lucky charm that a poker player uses to guard his hole cards.

CASINO – A building licensed for gambling.

CHALK – The favoured team in a sporting event.

CHECKING – In poker, a player checks when he wants to stay in the game, but doesn't want to bet. You can only check if no one has made a bet during the current round. Once a bet is made, you can call, raise or fold, but you can no longer check.

CHECK-RAISE – To not bet on a poker hand, in the hope that another player will bet and present you with an opportunity to raise. Players with strong hands use this gambit to bring additional chips into the pot.

CHEMIN DE FER – A similar game to baccarat.

CHOP – To split money in the pot – or even a tournament's prize pool – between two or more players.

CINCH – An unbeatable hand.

CIRCLE GAMES – A sporting event with limited action, typically due to injuries, weather conditions or other factors that make it an unstable play.

CLAIMING RACE – Horse races typically featuring the least impressive horses and the cheapest prize pools. Claimers are for sale at races at set prices. The claiming price puts a ceiling on the horses' values, ensuring that the race is evenly matched.

COFFEEHOUSING – Table talk, usually strategically orchestrated, to get a read on an opponent or to psych him out.

COLT – An uncastrated male horse aged four or younger.

COLUMN BET – A roulette bet on any of the numbers in one of the three roulette table's columns. (Pays 2–1.)

COMBINATION BET – Using one or more chips in the same position on a roulette table to bet on more than one number at a time.

COMBINATION TICKET – A keno ticket in which groups of numbers are bet several different ways.

COME BET – Betting in craps that the dice will pass, made after the come-out roll.

COME BOX – The area on the craps table layout where come bets are made.

COME-OUT ROLL – The initial or first roll of the dice in craps before any point has been established.

COME OVER THE TOP – To make a large re-raise at poker.

COMMUNITY CARDS – In poker, community cards

are cards that are dealt face up and shared by all players. In Texas Hold'em, for example, each player is dealt two face-down cards and the rest of their hands are composed of five face-up community cards.

COMPS – Complimentary gifts used by casinos to attract players.

COPY – When the player and the banker in pai gow poker have the same two-card hand or the same five-card hand. The banker wins all copies.

CORNER BET – One roulette wager on four numbers at a time. (Pays 8–1.)

COVER – In sports betting, a team covers by beating the spread by the required number of points.

COVERALL – A Bingo game in which the winner is the first person to fill every box on the card.

CRAP OUT – To throw a craps on the come-out roll, an automatic loser for pass line bettors.

CRAPS – In craps, this is the term for a roll of a 2, 3 or 12 (along with the name of the game) Also refers to the game itself.

CROUPIER – Person who works in a casino and deals cards, roulette and other games.

DAILY DOUBLE – A wager in which the bettor selects the winners of two consecutive races, typically the first two races of the day.

DAUBER – A device used to mark off numbers on a Bingo card as they are called out.

DEAD MONEY – A player who has no realistic chance of winning. Or money contributed to the pot by a player no longer in the pot.

DEALER BUTTON – See 'Button'.

DERIVATIVE – An investment, the underlying value of which depends on that of some other investments.

DON'T COME BET – A craps bet made after the come-out roll that the dice won't pass, betting against the dice.

DON'T COME BOX – The area on the craps table layout where don't come bets are made.

DON'T PASS BET – A craps bet made after the

come-out roll that the dice won't pass, betting against the dice.

DON'T PASS LINE – The area on the craps table layout where don't pass bets are made.

DOOR CARD – A player's first face-up card in a stud poker game.

DOUBLE DOWN – In blackjack, this is when you turn your cards face up, double your bet and receive one and only one more card.

DOZEN BET – A wager on 12 numbers on the roulette layout at the same time. The numbers are divided as such: 1–12, 13–24, and 25–36. (Pays 2–1.)

DRAW – The second round of cards dealt in draw poker. Also a situation in which you need one card in poker in order to make your hand. Generally refers to a player trying to complete either a straight or a flush. If you have four hearts after the flop, for example, you are on a flush draw.

DRAW BUTTON – In video poker, this button allows you to draw up to five new cards.

DRAW POKER – A poker game in which all cards are dealt face down.

DUMPING OFF – Intentionally losing hands in a poker tournament so that a compatriot can get your chips and have a better chance of winning.

EACH WAY – A bet in which the punter backs a horse to finish in the first three (sometimes four).

EARLY, MIDDLE AND LATE POSITIONS – Based on your seat at the table, and the position of the dealer's button, when you will bet or check or raise or fold. In an eight-handed game, the first three players to act are considered to be in early position, the next three are in middle position, and the final two are said to be in late position. Late position is the most desired of the three.

EASY WAY – In craps, this is a roll of a 4, 6, 8 or 10 when the dice are not matched as a pair.

EVEN MONEY – A wager in which neither opponent lays any odds.

EVEN-ODD BET – A roulette bet that either an even or odd number will come up. (Pays 1–1.)

EXACTA – A wager in which the bettor selects the top two finishers in a race (also known as a 'perfects').

EXPECTED WIN RATE – The percentage of the total amount of money wagered that you can expect to win or lose over a period of time.

FACE – Derisive term for poor player who loses lots of cash.

FAST RAIL – A bias in which horses running close to the rail have an edge over those farther away from the rail.

FAVOURITE – The event or hand that has the best mathematical chance of winning.

FIELD BET – A craps bet that the next roll of the dice will come up 2, 3, 4, 9, 10, 11 or 12.

FIFTH STREET – Third-round betting in seven-card stud, the fifth card on the board and the final round of betting in Texas Hold'em poker.

FILLY – A female horse, four years old or younger.

FINAL TABLE – The culmination of a tournament in which the remaining players compete against one another at a single table.

FIRST BASE – At the blackjack table, the position on the far left of the dealer, and the first person to be dealt cards.

FISH – A poor player who drops lots of cash.

FISHING – Staying in a poker game longer than you should because you're looking for the card that will make your hand a winner.

FLAT TOP – A slot machine with a fixed jackpot (as opposed to progressive).

FLOP – In Texas Hold'em poker, the second round of betting (following the blinds) starts after the first three community cards are dealt. These three cards are known as the 'flop'.

FOLD/FOLDING – In poker, a player folds by throwing away his cards. After folding, he makes no more bets on that hand, receives no more cards during the hand and cannot win the pot.

FOOTBALL POOLS – A form of gambling in which the punter fills in a coupon forecasting the results of football matches.

FORM – Predominantly a horse-racing term referring to the past performance of a horse.

FOURTH STREET – See 'Turn'.

FREE CARD – If none of the players bets during a given round, all players get to see the next card without having to put any money in the pot. So that card is considered 'free'.

FREEZE OUT – A poker tournament in which each player starts with the same amount of chips and continues until one player holds all the chips. The World Series adopted the freeze-out format in its second year, a move that helped spur on its popularity.

FRENCH/EUROPEAN WHEEL – A roulette wheel containing just one 0.

FRUIT MACHINE – A machine in which a player pulls a lever or presses a button to activate the reels, which often have fruits as symbols.

FURLONG – Track distance is measured in furlongs. One furlong is 220 yards. Eight furlongs is one mile.

FUTURE BET – A wager selected well in advance.

FUTURES – Making a contract to by or sell an investment or commodity at a fixed price on or before a specific date in the future.

GAMBLING COMMISSION – A government body in the UK set up in the new Gambling Act of 2005, which will come into effect in 2007.

GELDING – A castrated colt.

GIVE ACTION – To make bets in which you do not necessarily have an advantage – in the hope of loosening up tight players.

GRINDER – A gambler who employs a slow, conservative, methodical style of play, hoping to wear down opponents.

GUINEAS – The unit of currency still used to trade bloodstock (horses). A guinea is 5 per cent more than a pound (1.05) so 10,000 guineas is £10,500.

GUTSHOT – In poker, an inside straight draw. See 'Bellybuster'.

HANDICAP RACE – In handicap races, weights are allotted according to the rating assigned to the horse by the racetrack handicapper. The weight carried includes the jockey and additional weights in the saddlecloth (in case the jockey isn't heavy enough).

HANDICAPPER – A person who studies upcoming sporting events and rates them according to how he foresees the outcome.

HARD HAND – Any blackjack hand that doesn't contain an ace valued at 11 is a hard hand.

HARD WAY – In craps, this is a roll in which the dice come as a pair for the 4, 6, 8 or 10 (2-2, 3-3, 4-4 or 5-5).

HAZZARD – A gambling game similar to craps in which two dice are rolled – one of the most popular forms of gambling in the Regency period (1780–1830).

HEADS-UP – A game between only two players. The term is often used to describe tournament situations in which the field is down to a pair of contenders.

HEDGING – Placing bets on the opposite side to cut losses or guarantee winning a minimal amount of money.

HIGH-LOW BET – A roulette bet on either the high numbers (19–36) or the low numbers (1–18). (Pays 1–1.)

HI/LO SPLIT – A game in which the best high hand and the best low hand split the pot. It is a popular variation of seven-card stud and Omaha.

HIT – In blackjack, a hit is when the player takes another card.

HOLE CARD – In blackjack, the hole card is the card that's face down. You don't learn the value of the hole card until after you play your hand. (American blackjack only – the rules in Europe are different.) In poker, a player's face-down cards that no one else can see.

HOOK – A half point added to football and basketball betting lines, making it impossible to push.

HOUSE EDGE – The percentage of each bet that you make, on average, that the house takes in.

IN-RUNNING BET – A wager made on an event while the event is in progress.

INSIDE BET – A roulette wager placed on any individual number on the table, including 0 (or 00 in America), or any combination of the numbers.

INSIDE STRAIGHT – See 'Bellybuster'.

INSURANCE – In blackjack, insurance is a side bet that the dealer has a natural. It's only offered when the dealer's up card is an ace. If the dealer has a natural, the insurance bet wins double. If the dealer doesn't have a natural, the insurance bet loses.

JOLLY – The favourite.

JUICE – The bookmaker's commission. See also 'Vigourish'.

KENO BOARD – The board displaying winning keno numbers.

KICKER – Side card of the highest denomination. If you have a pair of Queens, an Ace, 10 and 8, you have a pair of Queens with an Ace kicker.

KNOCK-OUT – When a bookmaker extends the odds on an event purposely.

LAY BET – A craps bet in which a wrong bettor bets that a 7 will be rolled before the number (point).

LAY DOWN – To fold a strong hand when you think your opponent has a better one. Phil Hellmuth prides himself on making good lay-downs, and it is a cornerstone of his supertight strategy.

LAYING THE POINTS – Betting the favourite.

LIMIT – The maximum amount a bookmaker will allow you to bet before changing the odds and/or the points, or the 'cap' on what one person can wager.

LIMP-INS – Calling the big blind (forced opener) rather than raising in the first round of betting in poker.

LINE – The listed odds or points on a game.

LINEMAKER – The person who sets up the original and subsequent betting lines.

LIVE ONE – See 'Fish'.

LONG – Buying contracts for commodities or financial instruments in the futures market (opposite of short).

LOOSE – A player who plays a lot of hands and gets involved in a lot of pots.

LOTTERY – Gambling on a ticket that you purchase which is subsequently part of a prize draw.

LOW POKER – When playing low poker, the Ace is the lowest card and the lowest hand wins. The best possible hand you can have in low poker is A-2-3-4-5.

MADE HAND – A strong hand – say a flush or straight or full house – that is complete and not requiring any additional cards (even though there are more coming).

MAIDEN RACE – In racing, a maiden race is one in which none of the participating horses has ever won a race. Horses of both genders are allowed to participate.

MARE – A female horse, five years old or older.

MARGIN CALL – A call made by a broker to a client

when the margin held is below that necessary to maintain his contracts.

MARTINGALE SYSTEM – A well-known roulette staking system in which the player doubles his bets after each loss until he wins or reaches the table maximum.

MARKER – A signed promissory note through which casinos and card clubs provide cash for players.

MIDDLING – Winning both sides of a betting proposition. For example, betting the favoured team at -6.5 with one bookmaker and then taking the underdog at +7.5 with another bookmaker. If the favourite wins by 7 points, you win both bets. With all other outcomes you push.

MINI-BACCARAT – A scaled-down version of baccarat, played with fewer players and dealers; the rules are the same as baccarat.

MONEY MANAGEMENT – A term used to describe how a player handles his cash at the table and away from it – often referring to whether or not a successful player gambles away his bankroll at sucker games. 'You'll never see Barry Greenstein blowing his winnings at the craps table. He has excellent money-management skills.'

MOVE IN – When a player goes all-in with a raise, moving his entire chip stack into the pot.

MUCK – Fold.

NATIONAL LOTTERY – Reintroduced by the UK government in 1994 for the first time since 1826. It is a pool gamble, with the total sum gambled divided between the winners, Camelot, the licensee and good causes.

NATURAL – In blackjack, a natural is a two-card hand worth 21 points (the best possible score).

NO LIMIT TEXAS HOLD'EM – A form of poker using five community cards in with the pocket cards and no betting limits.

ODDS – The offer made in ratios by the bookmaker or other person laying bets. For example, 8–1, when a punter stakes 10 to win 80, or 6–4 where a punter stakes 10 to win 15. These are odds-against bets, expressed in traditional format. When the odds on offer are odds-on, the ratio is expressed in reverse, e.g. 4–6 or as 'Six to four on'. In this case, a gambler would need to stake 30, for example, to win 20. An interesting footnote to traditional odds is that they are quoted as 6–4 and 11–8, etc., because in pre-decimal money there were eight half crowns to a pound, and this made settling of bets easier.

ODDS-ON FAVOURITE – A team, animal or athlete so heavily favoured that the odds are less than even.

ODDSMAKER – Linemaker.

OFF SUIT – When two or more cards are of varying suits. If all four suits are visible, it is called a rainbow.

ONE-ROLL BET – A craps bet in which the outcome is determined by the next roll of the dice.

ON THE BUBBLE – When a player in a tournament is a place or two behind the point where cash prizes are given out. Let's assume a tournament pays the top 20 finishers, but there are 32 left and you're number 32. You might say, 'I'm on the bubble, but it won't affect my strategy. I'm still playing to win.'

ON TILT – The emotional mind of players who blow a couple of big hands, lose their composure and start making bad plays (usually being too aggressive, or playing like maniacs). As in: 'A few bad beats and Stu Ungar would go on tilt.' Also known as steaming.

OPENING – In poker, the player who bets first is opening.

OPEN-END STRAIGHT DRAW – The opposite of a gutshot or bellybuster, it's when you are one card away from hitting a straight from the top or bottom. If you hold 4-5-6-7, you are on an open-ended straight draw, as it'll be made with either a 3 or an 8.

OUTS – Number of unexposed cards that can turn your drawing hand into a made hand. If you hold an Ace and need another to win the hand, you have three outs if no other Aces are exposed on the table.

OUTSIDE BET – A roulette bet on red, black, odd, even, high or low.

OVERBROKE – When a bookmaker has priced up an event and the odds are less than 100 per cent, thereby theoretically allowing a punter to back every outcome and show a turn of profit.

OVERCARD – The highest card on the board.

OVERROUND – When a bookmaker has priced up an event and the odds exceed 100 per cent, giving the bookmaker a margin of profit.

OVER/UNDER – A wager in which you bet on whether the final score of a sporting event will be either higher or lower than a number specified by the oddsmaker.

PARI-MUTUEL – A French term that translates loosely to 'mutual stake'. Odds for a pari-mutuel betting system are determined by the bettors. The track takes a fixed percentage of the pot and the rest is divided among the winning bettors.

PARLAY – A bet in which wagers are made on several events and only pays out if each wager is successful. The advantage is a bigger payout. For example, a two-team parlay typically pays at 13–5 odds, a three-team parlay pays at 5–1 odds, a four-team parlay pays at 8–1 odds etc.

PASS LINE – The area on the craps table layout where pass-line bets are made.

PASS-LINE BET – A bet in craps that the dice will pass, betting with the dice.

PAST-PERFORMANCE SHEET – A compilation of data on horses based on recent races. The more experienced you get, the more you'll be able to read into a past-performance sheet and the more you'll be able to utilise it. Past-performance sheets serve as quick references to vital information about horses, such as how they do under certain track conditions and at what distance(s) they are most effective.

PAYLINE – The line on a slot machine on which the symbols from each reel must line up.

PAYOUT PERCENTAGE – The percentage of each dollar played in a video poker or slot machine that the machine returns to the player.

PAYOUT TABLE – A posting on the front of a video poker machine telling you what each winning hand pays for the number of credits played.

PENETRATION – The amount of cards in blackjack that are dealt before the dealer reshuffles all the cards in the shoe. The lower the penetration, the lower the chances of counting cards effectively.

PICK – A multi-race wager in which the winners of

all included races must be selected (e.g. pick three, pick six, pick nine etc.).

PICK'EM – A sporting event in which no team is favoured.

PIP – The suit symbols on a non-court card.

POCKET CARDS – The two cards dealt in Texas Hold'em that nobody else is entitled to see.

POINTSPREAD – The amount of points the bettor must give to wager on a game. If Team 1 is favoured and the point spread is 6.5, Team 1 must win by seven or more points to cover the pointspread.

POKER – Almost 200 years old, poker has become *the* popular and fashionable card game to play. The attraction of the game is that the best hand dealt can be outdrawn by an opponent, and contestants have to stake money to stay in the hand to its conclusion.

POOLS – Various forms of gambling in which all the bets made are aggregated and shared between the winners, less a fixed percentage for the organisers.

POST POSITION – The position in which a horse

starts a race. Post positions are numbered consecutively, with No.1 being closest to the rail.

POST TIME – The time at which a race starts. Horses line up at the starting gate one or two minutes before post time.

POT ODDS – The size of the pot divided by the cost of calling a bet. If it costs only $5 to possibly win a $100 pot, you are getting 20–1 odds.

PREMIUM BONDS – Government bonds that retain their face value, and pay out monthly prizes.

PROGRESSIVE – A slot or video poker game in which the potential jackpot increases with each credit that's played.

PROPOSITION BET – A wager on a particular aspect of an event, such as how many strikes a pitcher will throw or how many passes a quarterback will complete.

PUNTER – The most commonly used term to describe a gambler or bettor.

PUNTO BANCO – A variant of baccarat.

PURSE – In racing, a purse is the prize money that's distributed to the owners of the winning horses.

PUSH – A game in which neither side wins and all money is returned to the bettors. For example, if the Packers are favoured by 7 and they win by 7, the game is a push.

QUADS – Four of a kind.

QUARTER – A $25 chip or bet.

QUINELLA – A wager in which the first two finishers must be picked in either order.

RAFFLE – A gamble in which a large number of punters buy a ticket which is then mixed with other tickets, and a winning ticket drawn.

RAG – A small card that doesn't help your hand.

RAILBIRD – A spectator at a poker event. The name comes from the term 'rail', which is used to describe the waist-high divider that separates the players from the fans. When a player busts out of a tournament, the player goes to sit on the rail.

RAIL – The inside edge of a racetrack.

RAINBOW – Cards of different suits.

RAISE/RAISING – In poker, a player raises by matching the previous bet and then betting more, thereby increasing the stake for the remaining players.

RAKE – In poker, a rake is the money that the casino or card-room charge for each hand. It's typically a percentage or flat fee that's taken from each pot after each round of betting.

RAPIDO – A version of keno.

READ – To evaluate another player based on body language and betting patterns in order to make your best guess about the strength of their hand.

REBUY – To purchase another set of chips for use in a tournament. A select few events at the World Series permit rebuys in the first few hours of competition. In 2004, Daniel Negreanu set a record by rebuying 27 times in a $1,000 no-limit Hold'em event.

RED-BLACK BET – A roulette wager on either red or black. (Pays 1–1.)

RIVER – The final card dealt in a game of stud or Hold'em poker.

ROULETTE – A casino game in which a spinning ball is dropped into a numbered slot.

ROUNDER – A professional gambler who plays for high stakes and frequently travels the country to find the best game.

ROUND ROBIN – A parlay bet in which the bettor wagers various combining team wagers. A three-team robin, for example, consists of Team 1 vs. Team 2, 1 vs. 3, and 2 vs. 3.

SANDBAG – To hold back and call, even though you have a very good hand.

SCOOP – When you are playing Hi/Lo poker and you win with the high as well as the low. As in: 'Cyndy Violette scooped the pot with a 6 low and a flush.'

SEMI BLUFFING – Betting high with an unmade hand that has a reasonable chance of improving.

SET – Three of a kind in poker.

SEVENTH STREET – The fifth and final round of betting in seven-card stud. (Each player has seven cards.)

SHARP – A slang word in regular usage in the 18th century to describe a crafty gambler who takes advantage of a foolish punter.

SHOE – The box that holds the cards being dealt. Blackjack players who count cards in an effort to determine the likeliness of certain cards being dealt have a much higher success rate when there are fewer decks in the shoe. The amount of decks in the shoe typically varies from one to six.

SHORT – A term to describe a trade in the futures markets when you bet on the value of a commodity falling. The opposite to long.

SHORT-HANDED – A poker game with fewer than five players.

SHORT STACKED – A player with few chips in front of him.

SIX-NUMBER BET – An inside combination bet in roulette on six numbers at the same time.

SIXTH STREET – The fourth round of betting in seven-card stud. (Each player has six cards.)

SLOW PLAY – When you have a strong hand but pretend not to, to encourage others to bet more.

SLOW RAIL – A bias in which horses running further away from the rail have an advantage over horses running close to it.

SNAKE EYES – A craps term for the number 2.

SOFT HAND – In blackjack, any hand that contains an Ace that's valued at 1 is a soft hand.

SPEED RATING – Horses are assigned speed ratings based on their past performances. The lengths of races and the track conditions are taken into consideration upon the determination of this number. The speed rating relates how fast a horse ran to some standard that allows comparison between different past races.

SPLASH – Technically illegal but common. To throw your chips into the pot in a haphazard way and before anyone can verify the amount.

SPLASHY – A style in which you make lots of big bets.

SPLIT – In blackjack, players can split hands after two cards are dealt if the two cards are of the same value. Bets are automatically doubled when a player splits.

SPLIT BET – An inside combination bet in roulette on two numbers at the same time.

SPORTS BOOK – A online or offline facility that accepts wagers on sporting events.

SPREAD BETTING – Betting offered by firms where a customer is offered a spread of possibilities on an event, for example 48–54, being the time in minutes of the first goal in a football match. Punters who think that there will be a quick early goal would sell the index (go short) at 48, and punters who think there will be a late (or no goal) would buy (or go long) at 54. The payout, or loss, is determined by the make-up in time, and the size of the bet. In the above example, if a goal was scored at the 70th minute, the seller would pay £220 for a £10 bet, while the buyer would receive £160. The difference is the firm's margin.

SPREAD-LIMIT GAME – A poker game in which any bet between two limits is allowed at any time.

STAKE – The amount of money for which a bet is made.

STAKES RACE – In racing, stakes races attract the best horses and offer the largest purses. America's Triple Crown races – the Kentucky Derby, The Preakness and the Belmont Stakes – are examples of stakes races.

STAND – In blackjack, standing is when you don't take any more cards.

STANDOFF – A situation in craps in which no decision results from a throw of the dice in certain bets.

STEAL – A player is said to steal when winning a pot by bluffing. Often referred to in conjunction with blinds – when a player with low cards bets high before the flop and steals blinds.

STEAMROLL – To re-raise to make players call two bets instead of one.

STRAGGLERS – Early-position players who go for the minimum bet. Also known as limpers.

STRUCTURED GAME – Also known as the 'fixed-limit' game, a structured game is one in which the first dollar amount is what can be bet or raised in the early rounds, while the second amount is what can be raised in the later rounds.

STUCK – To be losing. As in: 'I can't go home now, not when I'm stuck $10,000.'

STUD POKER – A poker game in which certain cards are dealt face up, while the rest are dealt face down.

SUCK OUT – To win a hand after the flop despite poor odds of winning.

SUITED CONNECTORS – Sequential hole cards in the same suit.

SURRENDER – A rule in blackjack that allows players to bail out of a hand if it looks like they're going to lose. Surrendering players give up half their bets for the privilege of not playing out the hand.

SWEEPSTAKE – A form of betting in which the players bet the same amount and the winner takes all.

TABLE IMAGE – The way other players at the table see you. This may be inspired by your play or your overall persona.

TEASER BET – A bet in which the bettor is allowed to pad the point spread and/or over/under total to improve his chances of winning. The chances of winning are better, but the payouts are much lower.

TELL – An involuntary action that gives opponents clues about the cards another player is holding.

TEXAS HOLD'EM – The current most popular version of poker.

THE NUTS – An unbeatable hand in poker.

THIRD BASE – The nearest seat at a blackjack table to the right of the dealer. The player at third base is the last player to be dealt.

THIRD STREET – The first round of betting in seven-card stud. (Each player has three cards.)

TIGHT – A style in which you are extremely selective in choosing which hands to play. Phil Hellmuth is known for playing extremely tight.

TILT – Negative behaviour as a result of losing and attempting to recoup one's losses through bad play.

TOTE – A form of pool gambling on horses run by the government.

TOTE BOARD – A display of the totals bet on the various horses to win, place and show as well as the odds a bettor is likely to receive on win bets. Tote boards are typically updated in one-minute intervals before the start of a race.

TRIFECTA – A wager in which the bettor selects the first three finishers of a race in exact order.

TRIO BET – A combination bet in roulette on three numbers at the same time.

TRIPS – Three of a kind.

TURN CARD – The fourth community card.

UNDER – A bet that combined total points scored

by both teams during a game will be under a specified total.

UNDERDOG – The team or person picked by the oddsmakers to lose.

UNDER THE GUN – First player to bet or fold.

UP CARD – In blackjack, the up card is the card in the dealer's hand that is face up for all players to see before they play their hands.

VALUE BET – A bet in which your primary objective is to increase the size of the pot and not make your opponents fold.

VIGOURISH – The bookmaker's commission. Also known as 'vig' or 'juice'.

WHEEL – Ace through five, which in some Hi/Lo games can be played as the highest and lowest hand (a straight to the 5, and a perfect low).

WHIST – A card game in which the players play to win the most tricks. Very popular in the 18th century, especially among the European community in India where fortunes were won and lost at the whist tables.

WIN/PLACE/SHOW – A horse picked to win must finish first. A horse picked to place must finish first or second. A horse picked to show must finish first, second or third.

WIRED – Adjective used to describe the first two cards when they're a pair. As in: 'I started with wired Aces, but I couldn't catch a set.'

WISE GUY – A knowledgeable handicapper or bettor.

WRONG BETTOR – A craps bettor whose bets don't pass (against the dice).